THE RESPONSIBLE MANAGER

PRACTICAL STRATEGIES FOR ETHICAL DECISION MAKING

Michael Rion

1817

Harper & Row, Publishers, San Francisco

New York, Grand Rapids, Philadelphia, St. Louis
London, Singapore, Sydney, Tokyo, Toronto

FIRST EDITION

Library of Congress Cataloging-in-Publication Data

Rion, Michael.
    The responsible manager: practical strategies for ethical deci-
sion making/Michael Rion.—1st ed.
      p.   cm.
    Includes bibliographical references.
    ISBN 0-06-066864-4
    1. Business ethics.   2. Industrial management—Moral and
ethical aspects.   I. Title.
HF5387.R56   1989
174'.4—dc20   89-45187
                                                   CIP

---

90 91 92 93 94 WDR 10 9 8 7 6 5 4 3 2 1

This edition is printed on acid-free paper that meets the American
National Standards Institute Z39.48 Standard.

Contents

Preface

"We've got an order for a hundred gen set engines for Iran," drawled Harry over the phone on an autumn Friday afternoon in 1980. Iran was holding American hostages at the time, and economic sanctions by the United States were on again, off again. I squirmed as he pressed, "We're wondering whether Corporate Responsibility has any concerns about the sale. The distributor is eager for an answer, and the sale is worth well over a million dollars." Should we lose a million-dollar sale for moral qualms about dealing with Iran? Could the law and federal regulations answer the question? Should I give an immediate answer—as I sensed Harry wanted—or should I slow down the process and risk jeopardizing the deal?

Questions like these face managers like Harry and me every day. A marketing director worries whether a potential sale in a South American country might implicate her company in repressive police activities. Who can she talk to? What will they say? A personnel manager is puzzled whether a proposed compensation scheme is "fair." What does he understand fairness to mean? Meanwhile, a purchasing agent for the company wonders what to do about a proposed trip to visit a vendor's plant, all expenses paid. Does corporate policy tell him how to respond? Or does he simply rely on his own judgment? Not yet part of the company, a recently graduated MBA interviews for a financial analyst position. She wonders whether she wants to work in this kind of company. What are its values and how do they fit with hers? Can she make a career here without compromising her integrity?

As corporate responsibility officer for Cummins Engine Company, a Fortune 500 manufacturer of heavy-duty diesel engines, I spent four years struggling with questions like these and working closely with managers who live the questions daily. These managers carry out diverse tasks to accomplish corporate goals, such as meeting customer needs, strengthening an efficient manufacturing process, evaluating employee performance, and assessing risk and return on potential investments. I discovered that ethics is "baked into" their work. Questions of fairness emerge as part of the decision-making process on employee incentives; the meaning of promise keeping and trustworthiness is an integral part of the customer-supplier relationship; personal integrity and moral courage are essential ingredients in developing business relationships for the long term.

I also discovered some practical ways to help managers like Harry sort through such questions and find responsible patterns of action. There are no simple answers, or Harry would not have called me in the first place. And faithful, responsible persons can end up with different answers to tough questions; that is why, after a thorough assessment, Harry and I concluded the sale was acceptable, but a senior officer vetoed it on the grounds that our engines should not be in Iran while the country held American hostages.

Based on this intensive work in one company, and on wider experience in consulting with and teaching corporate executives in a variety of settings, I offer here an approach to ethics and management

- that is grounded in actual management practice;
- that provides helpful and practical ways of resolving ethical dilemmas in management; and
- that offers strategies for strengthening responsible management.

My hope is that you will find here a description of your world and of your questions of ethics that rings true, as well as practical help to resolve your questions of ethics.

Acknowledgments

I have been privileged, during the past ten years, to teach, consult, and work alongside hundreds of corporate managers. Without their willingness to share their concerns and to seek together to understand the meaning of responsible management, I would never have had the opportunity to learn about their world and to develop the ideas presented here.

More specifically, I am especially grateful to colleagues too numerous to mention at Cummins Engine Company in Columbus, Indiana, with whom I learned most directly about the texture of management ethics. Special thanks are due to Charles W. Powers and Timothy P. Gardner, who invited me to join them at Cummins, and to Michael F. Brewer, to whom I "reported" and with whom I honed my thinking in response to his probing questions. I also had the special privilege to work for J. Irwin Miller on several projects and, in the process, to learn much from his practical wisdom so evident in the quotations cited in this book.

Charles W. Powers and Jon P. Gunnemann have been my mentors in linking ethics to management, and I owe more to them than formal citations in the notes can suggest.

I am grateful to Hartford Seminary for providing sabbatical leave time during the summers of 1987 and 1988 during which I produced the manuscript. Karen Lebacqz and

Barbara G. Wheeler provided helpful encouragement in pursuing publication. Several managers read the manuscript and provided feedback, as did some academics and clergy. For their helpful advice and careful reading, I especially thank Sanford Cloud, Herbert Hansen, Frank Kirkpatrick, Alistair Longley-Cook, Ronald Woodruff, and members of Hartford Seminary's Public Policy Breakfast Group. My colleague at the seminary, Clifford Green, provided steady support and encouragement throughout the writing and publication process. Roland Seboldt's keen editorial advice and Joanne Sandstrom's copy editing are largely responsible for making the book more readable and accessible to the managers for whom it is written.

Without the skilled assistance of Roseann Lezak, Christine Meserve, and Teri Vaughn, these words would have been forever trapped in the electronic impulses of my computer disks. They patiently formatted, revised, printed, copied, and mailed numerous drafts.

Finally, I have written this manuscript in competition with my children—Carter, Cathy, and David—for space at the desk and access to the word processor, and I thank them for their patience and interest in their father's efforts. And with Nancy, who holds all of us together in our multiple family orbits, I celebrate again the meaning of commitment in the mutual love and responsibility of marriage.

CHAPTER ONE

Six Managers and Their Questions

Meet six managers with questions like yours.[1]

Charles Warren struggles with pressures to "play ball" by "fudging" on production reports to make the unit look better.

Carol Williams must make deep cuts in orders from a small, local machine shop whose proprietor appeals to her sense of loyalty.

Wendell Johnson believes it is time to fire an employee, but like all of us in that circumstance, he finds the decision painfully difficult.

Sharon Metzger helps the company fulfill its civic responsibilities, but a cynical old-timer raises new questions for her about the real nature of corporate philanthropy.

Steve Simpson is responsible for managing a plant closing and sale that will dramatically affect the local community.

Evelyn Bates faces the dilemma of many managers in international business about investments in South Africa and other trouble spots around the globe.

These six persons are typical of managers in many companies, large and small, and their questions are not at all unusual. To paraphrase a recent advertising campaign, they represent "real life, real questions." Here are their brief stories.

Charles Warren: "Playing Ball" with the Boss

Charles Warren[2] is a middle-aged engineer who works on new product introductions, a job that invites pressure for meeting deadlines from sales executives who are more concerned with their promised delivery dates than with the problems of engineers and plant personnel trying to get the product developed and manufactured. Charles recognizes the problems of being the bearer of bad news in this environment, and he believes the corporate atmosphere is increasingly unsympathetic to explanations for product delays. He often experiences questions of ethics in this setting:

> [M]anagement above me has lied, outright purposeful lies, primarily to other individuals within the company with respect to commitments that had been made. . . . Maybe . . . all you have to do is be quiet and it goes by. Or maybe you are forced to cover up for what has been said. . . . [I]t's one of those instantaneous kinds of things where I feel the jeopardy to me, personally, could be very great were I to go contrary to what was being said by the boss.[3]

He cites one particular example when the unit could look much better on internal reports if it "fudged a bit" in overstating what had actually been shipped by a certain date. Charles tried to present accurate data but was told to use different figures to make the reports look better. He recognizes that, despite the pressure from above, he is partially responsible for the misleading reports.

As he discusses this dilemma, Charles gives evidence of his own struggle with the tension between the clear duty to provide honest information and the equally clear threat to his own position if he fails to go along. On the one hand, he suggests that he does not want "to be any less ethical here at work than I am at home. I try to conduct myself in the same manner, no matter what."[4] Yet he also recognizes that the decision is, to some degree, out of his hands and that the misleading reports do not "matter all that much anyway." The customer is still served well enough, but the department looks better on paper. Furthermore, "[I]f you are in a position of jeopardy with your management, and if you are not dealing with something that's illegal, it's difficult not to want to play ball."[5]

Carol Williams: Cutting Orders, Cutting Ties

Responsible for purchasing decisions for an important product line in her company's main manufacturing plant, Carol Williams is a veteran of twenty-three years in the production side of a heavy equipment manufacturer. That experience has made her especially able to judge the capacities of suppliers to meet commitments, and she has, over the years, developed solid relationships with some loyal people in area machine shops. But those relationships can be painful as well, as she recently experienced during a severe downturn in orders for the product line she services.

Fred Perkins, vice-president for purchasing and Carol's immediate supervisor, had reviewed the numbers with her, and they were grim. Production normally at 300 units a day had already fallen to 250, and current projections of falling demand necessitated a further reduction to 200 units for the foreseeable future. The implications were widespread in the plant, because at least a hundred workers would be laid off indefinitely, and orders with suppliers had to be reduced as well. Carol spent the rest of the day reviewing commitments and standing orders with the thirty-six major suppliers she dealt with, finishing up with instructions for her staff to notify each of the suppliers about reductions in orders.

The next afternoon, Carol received the phone call she had half expected from Mel Thompson, owner of Thompson Metals, a small machine shop that had supplied the company with a key component over the years. "Carol, how can you do this to me? We have geared so much of our work to your company that we can't take a cut in orders like this without serious losses. This ain't no big time corporation, this is me and my boys, and we don't have other business to turn to!"

Carol explained the difficult situation in her own plant and added, "Mel, this isn't just a problem for you. We're having to cut orders across the board from all our suppliers."

Mel knew how to reach Carol's concern behind this policy statement. "Carol, we're not just another supplier; you and I go back almost twenty years. How many times have we worked extra fast to help you meet a new problem? Remember when we helped you solve that design problem on the fasteners? Probably saved your company thousands of dollars in fancy engineering consultant fees. And, besides, you know Sally is ailing and I've got to keep the shop going just to make ends meet. It's not fair to treat us like some of those big vendors out of Chicago. Don't our relationship count for something?"

Carol promised to call Mel back the next day. She went

home that evening still struggling with a question of ethics: Was it unfair to cut the orders to Mel's shop? She wondered whether there might be other options. She also worried whether her anxiety was a result of letting sentiment get in the way of business realities. Or did the relationship, indeed, count for something?

Wendell Johnson: Firing Is Never Simple

Wendell Johnson is a field engineer; his group is responsible for fixing product problems at the customer's site.[6] Technical knowledge and competent performance are critical to the group's success. The customer expects nothing less, and when a problem requires changes by other departments in the company, only irrefutable data will overcome their natural resistance. Good interpersonal skills help immensely, too, in accomplishing his unit's goals.

Wendell is struggling with an employee named Mac, a sixty-one-year-old who has been with the company for less than five years and is therefore not vested in the pension plan. Mac's performance is lackluster at best; indeed, Wendell can offer a litany of problems.

> [H]e has no knowledge of service delivery; his interpersonal skills require major development; his technical knowledge base does not exist. . . . [H]e lacks most, if not all, of the leadership qualities. He doesn't listen. He doesn't think about what other people are doing or feeling. . . . He has no common sense and is totally impractical. . . . Making it worse, he is overpaid for his contribution.[7]

Despite this extraordinary indictment of Mac's capacities, Wendell does "see value" in Mac for the company. He is good at developing standards and tests for quality control and has the necessary related theoretical and documentation skills.

But Wendell believes Mac must improve or be terminated. When he asked for help from personnel, one staff group recommended termination, while another suggested giving Mac another chance. Wendell bristles at the latter suggestion as he recounts the numerous chances he has already given Mac. These include several checkpoints over the past two years when Mac was warned about his performance, as well as specific goal setting and monitoring to be sure Mac understood his responsibilities. Most recently, Wendell spent an hour a week with Mac to discuss his work and to address specific problems. In some frustration, Wendell exclaims:

> I have met all the requirements of my ethics. The man will be terminated July 1 if he has not found another job in the company. He doesn't know that exactly. He knows that by July 1 he'd better be performing or have found another job or else. I haven't said explicitly that he will be fired July 1.[8]

Despite this strong judgment, Wendell still struggles. "The tough question is, do I terminate the individual?" Wendell believes Mac has something to offer the company and has sought to place him elsewhere. He worries whether he is being too harsh on Mac, as one personnel representative suggests. As he continues to debate himself, the questions of ethics troubling Wendell include fairness and simple human sensitivity to someone in difficulty.

> The issue I'm struggling with at this point is balancing what's the best thing for the employee and what's best for the organization. I think I have made the decision. . . . Anyway, the guilt trip is over. He performs or he's fired. It's

simple. Except that it won't be that simple. It's just easy to say.[9]

Sharon Metzger: Doing Good the Right Way

Sharon Metzger is public affairs manager for a medium-sized financial services company in a metropolitan area in the Midwest. Her responsibilities include managing the company's annual United Way drive and providing staff support to the Corporate Public Affairs Committee (CPAC), a group of senior officers who determine policies on corporate contributions to charitable causes. The company has a reputation as a socially responsible firm with generous gifts to community charities and an unusually high per capita giving rate to United Way. Indeed, the company has led its division in this category for four straight years.

Sharon moved into this position from public relations only nine months ago with enthusiasm for the company's commitment to public service. She still believes in that commitment, but she has found that "doing good" has its questions of ethics, too. As she prepares for her first annual report to the CPAC and her own subsequent performance review with the vice-president for human resources, she puzzles over two particular problems and whether to raise them with the CPAC.

Both problems emerged in a sobering conversation with Gene Costa, a financial analyst who has been with the company for many years. Gene is generally regarded as the company "sage," although most people advise taking his cynicism with a grain of salt.

"Are you getting your way with the United Way drive?" Gene asked with a hint of sarcasm.

Sharon felt defensive but replied that, yes, the drive was going well. "In fact," she said with growing fervor, "I think we'll lead in our division again this year."

"It isn't any wonder," replied Gene, "when supervisors check up on their employees about giving. I wonder why we don't just build a contribution percentage into each person's job description!"

Sharon countered that supervisors were asked not to apply pressure and that the amounts contributed were known only to a few people in accounting.

Gene laughed. "What you don't know doesn't hurt you, I guess. With the clear message about United Way leadership that Pat [the chief executive officer (CEO)] gives, people know what counts."

Before she could press Gene on his meaning, he changed the subject, but only in a way. "Besides, that's only one example of the way senior management uses company giving to enhance its own reputation and pet projects. Why, that grant you worked on to help build the new art museum exhibit hall was nothing more than dues for letting Pat chair the Art Board these last five years. And the grant to Hilson School over in Garden City has nothing to do with priorities; it was simply something Harry [the chief financial officer] wanted to do for his alma mater.

"You're a good person, Sharon, and you're doing a good job. But don't be so naive. You don't develop a public affairs giving program, you simply help senior management do what they want to do with some of the shareholders' money!"

Sharon sat stunned as Gene left her office. Was he right? Maybe not, because United Way is certainly a good cause, and surely top management has some discretion in making charitable contributions. On the other hand, there had to be limits on what the company could ask of people in personal giving. And what does it say about the company's values and commitments if corporate contributions merely represent the whims of senior management?

Steve Simpson: Closing Down

When Steve Simpson joined Sun Ship, situated outside Philadelphia in Chester, Pennsylvania, as general counsel in 1978, he discovered a once mighty shipbuilding firm in an advanced stage of decline.[10] A subsidiary of the Sun Company, a petroleum firm, Sun Ship suffered from keen international competition; its work force—35,000 at World War II—had shrunk to 4,200, and the shipyard was a financial drain on the parent company. Business strategies to concentrate on certain specialized shipbuilding roles generated hopes for a turnaround at the time of Steve's arrival, but these quickly evaporated in the face of stiff competition. In a particularly vivid example, Steve cites a shipbuilding contract in which the foreign competitor's bid for the entire project was less than Sun's cost for the steel alone.[11]

As a result, the parent company decided to close Sun Ship. Community leaders were critical of the business judgment involved in this decision because the company had no prior consultation with outsiders. Nevertheless, Steve argues that the decision had not been reached through a callous, unfeeling process.

> It was probably the most painful period of time that any of the decision makers experienced in their business lives, because . . . we all knew people who had worked there for three generations. . . . It was always with doubt: Are we doing the right thing? It was Thursday nights at ten o'clock at night. . . . It was Sunday morning telephone calls. . . . It was—for the people who had to make the [decision]— very, very painful.[12]

Once the decision to close was reached, Steve was responsible for managing the closing. A buyer would ultimately be found for a much smaller shipbuilding firm, but more than three thousand would lose their jobs. Steve was concerned for them, as well as about the impact of Sun's demise on Chester. Severance arrangements were developed in consultation with nonunion employees and, as required by contract, in negotiation with labor union representatives. These arrangements included lump-sum payments, early retirement plans, educational opportunities, career counseling and job placement services, and extended medical and life insurance benefits.

Community task forces were convened to assess the impact of Sun's decline. Following these discussions, Sun offered to make payments in lieu of taxes for three years to offset the loss of wage taxes from laid-off workers and to cover United Way pledges for a two-year transition period. A grant of $360,000 from Sun funded an economic development project aimed at stimulating new businesses in Chester. Not everyone agreed that these responses were sufficient or satisfactory—"there was no shortage of hands that were seeking for us to provide them with the means to solve their own real problems"—[13] but many former employees and community leaders applauded this response to the impact on the community.

Steve Simpson lived through questions of competing claims in this experience. He recognized the human dilemma of facing up to these claims and relationships while fulfilling his management role.

Q: Did the phasedown decision bother you a lot?

A: Sure. Sure. I had social friends who had worked at the shipyard during the Second World War. My father had friends who had worked at the shipyard before that. My father's first job was in Chester as a pharmacist. His first pay was a gold coin, and the guys from the shipyard used to go buy pharmaceuticals. Sure, it hurt. I had a personal tie to Sun Ship, as do most Philadelphians.

Q: How do you sort that out?

A: That's the essence of being a businessman.[14]

Evelyn Bates: To Invest or Not to Invest

As vice-president of Omega Division, Evelyn Bates oversees a relatively independent subsidiary of a large, multinational office technology company. In the early 1980s, she authorized a team to explore a manufacturing license agreement in South Africa after a government agency approached Omega with a highly attractive offer to allow a government-owned company to manufacture a profitable line of Omega's office equipment. The license would guarantee Omega a good royalty fee as well as provide further penetration in South Africa's growing office equipment market. And the deal would be financed by South African sources.

Evelyn knew about the controversy over U.S. corporate involvement in South Africa. Her genuine question was whether this particular business opportunity was morally appropriate or not. On the one hand, conversations with Omega's public affairs staff raised qualms about the deal. In the contemporary political scene, argued Jeff Seltzer from the corporate staff group, any new entry by U.S. companies would send a signal of support for the white regime. "Omega should not be in South Africa and, besides," argued Jeff, "it would probably generate public relations and shareholder problems that we don't need right now."

On the other hand, Evelyn knew that this particular

project would generate new jobs for unemployed and disenfranchised "coloureds" in the Cape Province. Furthermore, Omega's office equipment could be used in countless offices by blacks who were slowly working into the ranks of office workers. Why would an innocent office equipment venture providing good jobs ally Omega with the government's apartheid policy? Moreover, the deal was a very good business arrangement virtually guaranteed to boost Omega's profitability. "Omega is a business, not an emissary of American foreign policy," she told Jeff. "Aren't we reaching beyond our role when we try to make social-political decisions?"

As she talked further with Jeff, Evelyn also stumbled onto apparent contradictions that bothered her even more. "You mean the Computer Division has signed deals with Bulgaria and the People's Republic of China? Those are repressive Communist regimes! And, now that I think of it, our service contract with the Mexican banks does not exactly ally the company with a democratic government!" Jeff suggested that circumstances were different in each of these countries, but Evelyn's retort came spontaneously: "How can we be so self-righteous and inconsistent? If repression is bad in South Africa, it's bad everywhere! I wonder if we're just fooling ourselves with all this talk about responsibility in South Africa. Maybe we should just do business and leave politics to politicians."

Following her conversation with Jeff, however, Evelyn continued to worry about the South African deal. She wanted to do the right thing and to feel clearly that she had done so. But her own retort to Jeff was too simple, for she knew that moral concerns such as apartheid were directly relevant to the Omega manufacturing project. In the next week, she had to decide whether to approve the steps leading to establishing the licensing agreement. Her questions of ethics were still unresolved.

Answering Questions, Making Decisions: A Simple Framework

Questions of ethics like those confronting Evelyn and Steve, Carol and Wendell, and Charles and Sharon confront all managers. Decisions must be made to keep the organization moving. But ethical questions can be emotional, raising feelings not easily assessed or discussed in a business setting. This anxiety can paralyze the decision process or lead some managers to set aside ethics completely rather than deal with the passion beneath the surface. To make matters worse, many managers lack the language and practical concepts to enable them to assess ethical questions with confidence.

Six questions provide a useful framework for moving beyond concern and confusion to practical and responsible decisions. When a manager is faced with ethical dilemmas, careful attention to these six questions leads to a thoughtful resolution—not *the* right answer, but an ethically sensitive and well-considered judgment.

1. **Why is this bothering me?** Is it really an issue? Am I genuinely perplexed, or am I afraid to do what I know is right?
2. **Who else matters?** Who are the stakeholders who may be affected by my decisions?
3. **Is it *my* problem?** Have I caused the problem or has someone else? How far should I go in resolving the issue?

4. **What is the *ethical* concern**—legal obligation, fairness, promise keeping, honesty, doing good, avoiding harm?
5. **What do others think?** Can I learn from those who disagree with my judgment?
6. **Am I being true to myself?** What kind of person or company would do what I am contemplating? Could I share my decision "in good conscience" with my family? with colleagues? with public officials?

Using these questions as a checklist will help to resolve questions of ethics in management. In the next chapters, we will see how these questions help our six managers better understand and resolve their ethical concerns. And we will learn how to use the framework to address our own challenges as well.

But, What Is Ethics?

But what are we talking about? The very term *ethics* sometimes gets in the way of resolving the questions. To some, it connotes an absolutist, rigid set of constraints that violates our sense of independent judgment; to others, it may seem altogether too personal a topic for open discussion in the workplace. Still other managers may believe that ethics are simply subjective value judgments, that all of us have our own perspectives, and that there is no way to reconcile differences. The chapters that follow will dispel these misconceptions, but a preliminary definition of ethics may be helpful at the outset.

Ethics derives from the Greek word from which we get *ethos*, that is, from the notion of character and deep values that determine the identity and goodness or badness of an individual or group. Likewise, *moral* comes from the Latin root *mores,* that is, the customs and accepted rules of a group or society. Although the two terms, *ethics* and *morality,* are sometimes distinguished, they are basically synonyms pointing to standards of what is right and good.

Most of us have "built-in" ethical responses. We identify certain actions as wrong, others as morally praiseworthy. A public official lies about some action, and we say he was wrong to do so. Even if we excuse this behavior as a concession to "politics as a dirty business," our very awareness that an excuse is necessary reveals deeply held perceptions of what constitutes ethical behavior. A traditional value such as honesty—and others such as promise keeping, truth telling, justice, benevolence—endures because it is essential to the social fabric of human existence. Without certain fundamental principles of fair dealing and mutual respect, business would be impossible. Consider how chaotic business life would be if we could not generally count on associates, customers, and suppliers to keep their promises and to speak truthfully to us. We too easily forget how vital to daily existence are these usually unstated norms. But when the norms are violated—when a supplier, for example, proves unreliable in keeping to agreed-upon delivery schedules—we are abruptly reminded of their significance.

Imagine a baseball game in which the umpire arbitrarily awards a batter a fourth strike just because he feels like it or because he feels sorry for the batter caught in a slump! The opposing manager will first appeal to the rules of the game, but obviously it does not matter in the larger scheme of things whether the batter is out after three or four strikes. What matters is that the umpire has promised to officiate at the game by the agreed rules. The frustrated manager might well exclaim, "If you can't keep your promises, we can't play the game at all!" Basic moral principles such as honesty and fairness are essential to the very possibility of developing a game. Likewise, we can never get a human community going, whatever its peculiar modes of organization, without moral principles that create the possibility for dependable mutual relations.

Ethical principles do "work." But more is at issue here than mere pragmatism. As one philosopher put it, we should always treat persons as ends and never merely as means. Simply as fellow creatures, all human beings deserve our respect. To treat another person as a means to our own ends or to abuse his or her concerns and expectations out of carelessness is to deny that person the respect we expect for ourselves. This means that categories like human pain and misery, self-realization and happiness are ethical considerations. Ethical principles are essential to human interaction precisely because they embody the respect for persons that enables all parties involved to participate in the fabric of human community with dignity.

Questions of ethics that arise in management reflect this deeply rooted appreciation for mutual responsibility in community. Furthermore, when we consider particular principles, we typically recognize that ethical principles have significant authoritative guidance. If we are told an action is odd, or unwise, or unprofitable, we may resent the criticism, but we are not stung by it in the way we are when told our action is immoral. Moral principles have a special claim on us, symbolized by the notion of conscience. For many of us, this claim is grounded in religious convictions about the relationship of morality to the divine will. Others root the claim in respect for human dignity or simply in the powerful psychological effects of their upbringing. Whatever the source, most persons experience ethical guidelines as significant imperatives for their own action.

These are the considerations that move us to recognize and to puzzle or agonize over particular questions of ethics. Ethics is already "on the table" for most managers because ethics is so much a part of our common life, in business as well as in other arenas.

CHAPTER TWO

Why Is This Bothering Me?
Duties, Puzzles, and Competing Claims

Charles Warren is clearly bothered by the pressures on him to provide less-than-honest production reports. His discomfort is painful and his dilemma real. If he were to take a stand against his superiors, he might well risk his career opportunities and perhaps even his job.

Carol Williams is bothered, too, but not by threats or patterns of questionable activity. She is, rather, genuinely puzzled and torn about Mel Thompson's plaintive appeal, "Don't our relationship count for something?"

And Evelyn Bates worries about the right course of action concerning the South African project. The claims of different groups and different arguments echo in her mind as she prepares to make a decision about the license agreement.

All of them would do well to ask carefully, "Why is this bothering me?" as a first step in their efforts to resolve their concerns. Is the problem really an ethical issue?

Sometimes the answer is "no." We may see ethical problems even where they do not exist. Employees may be upset about top management's "perks," for example, assuming that a vice-president used the company plane for a personal jaunt when the trip was, in fact, a business assignment. Concerns about travel, meals, and entertainment often raise ethical questions, focused on possible conflicts of interest and compromise of business judgment on the part of one who accepts special treatment. But sometimes the concerned individual learns that the benefit being offered (for instance, an all-expense-paid trip to a vendor's plant site) is legitimate and acceptable to company policies. If managers err, it is better that they do so in favor of seeing ethical issues. But asking "Why is this bothering me?" may help to restrain over-zealous interpretations of ethics.

The question may also clarify the problem. Charles Warren clearly recognizes that he has an ethical duty to provide honest reporting, yet he appears to deceive himself with rationalizations. He suggests that the misleading reports do not matter very much and that he is, after all, a decent person trying to live with consistent moral principles both on and off the job. If he could explore with greater candor what bothers him, he might admit that the ethical responsibility is quite clear. He could then acknowledge that what bothers him is the difficulty of meeting the ethical obligation, not for any fault of his own but because of the environment in which he works. That recognition may not diminish his understandable discomfort, but it would focus his energy and imagination on considering ways to change the environment, on ways to limit his complicity, and on how and whether he should draw the line despite the great risks. These are all important and difficult tasks, and they are not accomplished so long as Charles lets himself assume that the ethical obligation is itself open to question.

The question "Why is this bothering me?" also helps Carol Williams and Evelyn Bates focus attention on the nature of their problems. Although ethical concerns can sometimes seem complex and multifaceted, Carol will likely recognize that what bothers her is the meaning of commitment in customer-supplier relations, specifically, her company's relationship with Thompson Metals. To be sure, other principles and relationships—for example, obligations to shareholders and employees and fairness to other suppliers—are in the background. But what really concerns Carol and what she needs to focus on most immediately is the meaning of this particular relationship. And it really is an issue, for it is not patently obvious to Carol what action would be most ethical.

Evelyn Bates, on the other hand, is likely to find that the more she defines what bothers her, the more it looks like a complex web of competing claims that she must somehow resolve. Potential employees would be benefited by the new venture, but other coloureds and blacks might see such new business as playing into the hands of the white government. Shareholders will benefit if the deal is financially sound, but other shareholders may challenge the company's entry into South Africa on social-political grounds. These competing claims are probably represented forcefully by Evelyn's immediate management colleagues as they argue their case. She has a genuine ethical dilemma on her hands, one that is complex and multifaceted.

Types of Ethical Issues

The problems facing Charles, Carol, and Evelyn illustrate three broad categories of ethical issues experienced by managers. The first type concerns a problem in which the ethical obligation itself is clear, although the choices involved may be tough ones for other reasons, as in Charles Warren's dilemma. A second type concerns a problem in which the nature of the ethical obligation is not so obvious, although it is clearly concentrated on a single principle or relationship. Carol's dilemma in deciding how far her commitment to Thompson Metals should go falls into this category, as does the general problem of being fair to particular employees in performance assessment. A third type concerns the problems that arise when multiple relationships and principles give rise to competing claims among a variety of interested parties and/or among two or more distinct ethical principles. Policy issues concerning investments in troubled countries overseas, such as Evelyn's decision, or plant closings are familiar examples here.

Remembering these three types can help you to sort out what bothers you and to focus your thinking and action. While many issues will have characteristics of all three types, typically the heart of the matter will lie in only one. Attention to examples in each category will make these distinctions more useful in practical applications.

1. Clear Duties

Across a wide range of business activities, we encounter ethical obligations that are unambiguous.

"Can I take home a box of floppy disks for the kids' games?"
"Those disks are for company, not personal, use!"

"Should we agree to a price-fixing offer?"
"Of course not."

"Will you accept a special favor to give my company the contract?"
"No!"

"I wonder if we could deceive the buyer by substituting a lesser quality product in the shipment?"

"No, we don't do business that way."

"Maybe I can overstate my trip expenses to gain a little extra cash."

"You know that would be wrong."

But if the ethical answers are so obvious, why do managers often experience the questions as dilemmas? Aside from those who simply ignore ethical behavior because of personal greed, right action is sometimes easier to talk about than to do, even for persons with high moral standards.

Sometimes it is quite clear what is right, but not at all clear how to do it. William Diehl, a former Bethlehem Steel executive, reports an incident early in his manufacturing career when a counterpart in another company called to suggest a price-fixing agreement; the caller suggested that Diehl's failure to help would lead the caller to lose everything and even to take his own life. " 'How can a young man like you live with yourself knowing that you are destroying me?' "[1] Price fixing was wrong, Diehl knew, but as a young manager he did not know how to deal with this coercive and manipulative caller.

In many such cases we are genuinely puzzled about questions of ethics, not because the ethics are in question, but because we are unsure what steps to take to fulfill the ethical obligation. Some companies seek to help employees challenge unethical behavior witnessed within the company and to raise such challenges without risk to their own careers. But effective procedures to make good on such protection require careful development. Even then, it is not always clear that formal procedures can protect the internal "whistleblower" from informal retaliation from a powerful antagonist. Other examples abound, such as how to discipline ethical failures effectively, when to use specific policy directions and when to rely on managerial discretion, or what to do when a manager happens to learn that a supplier or customer is engaged in unethical behavior.

Especially difficult are occasions when the ethics are clear, but you can do the right thing only at great personal risk within the company. A story about Nikita Khrushchev answering an anonymous written question at a press conference dramatizes the point.

> The question: What was he, an important figure, doing during all those crimes of Stalin he had retroactively exposed and denounced? Khrushchev was livid with rage. "Who asked that question?" he demanded. "Let him stand up!" Nobody did. "That's what I was doing," said Khrushchev.[2]

Some of the most anguishing ethical questions in organizations arise when an individual senses or actually experiences threats when he or she seeks to fulfill an ethical obligation or to call attention to unethical behavior. One well-known example is the story of Kermit Vandivier, a B. F. Goodrich data analyst, who raised questions about falsified reporting on tests of an aircraft brake assembly and ultimately lost his job.[3] The case is often cited because here an employee pursued an ethical obligation (to assure accurate test data and, more broadly, to prevent an unsafe brake from going into production) only to have his concerns suppressed and his career cut short. Less dramatic examples occur every day as individuals struggle with overbearing supervisors who push for special favors or lax standards, managers in one area witness suspect behavior in another unit but fail to act for fear of reprisals from a competitive unit, and senior people send signals to subordinates that bad news is not welcome news. The ethics may be clear, but the dilemmas of conscience and moral courage related to acting ethically are painfully difficult.

A variation on this theme is worth noting. Sometimes individuals conclude that they can no longer in good conscience continue working for a company. Perhaps a series of incidents confirms a growing suspicion that "this company is not my kind of company." Or a particular product or business decision becomes the key issue, as when a company increases its defense business or invests in a country governed by a repressive regime in ways that conflict with the individual's values. Although persons of goodwill might disagree about the ethical judgment, the individual sees a clear ethical duty to leave but agonizes over the consequences to self and family of following through on the implications of that moral judgment.

2. Single Principle/Single Relationship

If we sometimes experience questions of ethics with clear answers, just as often we are puzzled about what is, indeed, the right choice or course of action.

"Is it fair to deal with these two customers differently?"

"Is it wrong to tell the customer 'half-truths' in the midst of our negotiations over price?"

"How much should we do for the merchants dislocated by our new office construction?"

"Does this employee deserve another chance, or is it time to terminate?"

Business opportunities pose choices and pressures to act in certain ways, and morally good individuals are often genuinely unclear about the nature and extent of their ethical obligations. Although there are sometimes a number of relationships and ethical principles at stake, very often the concern and puzzlement focuses on one central relationship and/or the meaning of one key ethical principle. The most typical principles in such cases are fairness, honesty, commitment, and avoiding harm.

The moral notion that probably emerges most frequently in management is fairness. What could be more basic than to treat people fairly? We share this commitment, but we find the meaning of fairness less than obvious in specific cases. Often the question concerns employee relationships and personnel policies. What constitutes fair treatment for Martha on this job with her particular abilities in comparison with Fred on another job with his experience and capacities? When is differential treatment unfair, and when are exceptions the only way to provide genuinely fair treatment? If you supervise even one employee, you wonder about the specific meaning of fairness on a regular basis. It may be in response to complaints about workload or compensation, or it may arise from your own concerns as the annual performance review and subsequent compensation adjustments come around.

Fairness to employees, then, routinely emerges as an ethical question in regular management responsibilities. In addition, new challenges and difficulties may pose special questions of fairness that are especially puzzling because so much human pain may be involved. The opportunities and pressures associated with affirmative action are a good example; managers in good conscience struggle to understand what is fair in the treatment of both new and different people and continuing workers. Or, if wages and salaries must be cut because of external pressures on costs, what is fair in allocating the cuts? The options may be narrow, as when collective bargaining agreements dictate certain steps such as layoffs, or they may include broader opportunities such as shared salary reductions. Even for those terminated, there are questions of continuing benefits, severance pay, and the extent of outplacement services provided. Responsible managers worry over such decisions and about the meaning of fairness to their employees.

And fairness applies to others, too. Often the relationships to customers and suppliers are especially important to managers in marketing or purchasing, and they wonder about fair treatment here as well. Even within the framework of legal guidance, questions may arise about what differences in treatment are justified on such matters as pricing, bidding, and sharing product information. If a company works closely with one supplier to develop a product and then takes the specifications to a second supplier who can manufacture it more cheaply, what counts as fair treatment for the first supplier who devoted significant development costs to the project? If one customer negotiates a good deal on a particular wholesale order, is it fair not to offer the same terms to a competitive customer? What is fair treatment to a small supplier with a long relationship to a company when the company experiences a downturn and threatens to cut orders to an extent that devastates the supplier? Here, again, the ethical question focuses primarily on the meaning of this one principle in this particular relationship, despite the fact that many other considerations (such as profitability and commitments to employees) are in the background of the decision.

Another principle that often emerges in managerial life is honesty. No one wants to be dishonest, yet the exact moral meaning of truthfulness in particular cases is not always obvious. This is evident when managers from different departments in the same company discuss moral guidelines for negotiating. What counts as deception? How is it distinguished from the acceptable "puffery" recognized by all parties as part of the negotiating "game"? Those who negotiate regularly in tough, competitive situations are likely to respond differently than employees with staff responsibilities, who are removed from the actual negotiating experience. The desire to be honest may be shared, but what the principle means in practical circumstances with particular customers or competitors may be less clear.

Similar questions arise in developing product information for advertising and other marketing purposes. How much information is enough for truthful communication? If we know the product has some potential problems, should we volunteer this information? Regulatory agencies often require product information. Is the same standard of truthfulness applied to both marketing and regulatory communications? This question is not rhetorical; individual managers often worry about just such concerns, and they may disagree with one another across organizational boundaries (engineers, for instance, may be more inclined to share detailed data about problems than are marketing representatives). In such cases, the question of ethics very often turns on understanding what honesty means in a particular circumstance and set of relationships.

Honest communication is also a critical ethical dimension of employee relations. At the supervisory level, this is evident in the challenge to provide honest feedback in the performance review process. Throughout the organization, honesty is often an issue in communications to employees about business conditions. How much should senior management share, and when, about business plans and contingencies when the environment is rapidly changing and competitors have an alert ear to the ground to anticipate what the company may do? This ongoing question about honest communication becomes acute when a company contemplates closing a plant or unit. Indeed, a recent federal statute and some state laws governing plant closings legislate the meaning of honesty with requirements for advance notice.

Another key ethical principle that often emerges in the midst of management is promise keeping or the meaning of commitment in business life. As with fairness and honesty, concern for commitment often springs from personal relationships in the managerial context. For instance, some managers will struggle with their obligations to long-term employees when performance problems are identified in individual cases or when widespread layoffs are considered in economic downturns. Does the commitment of the loyal employee over the long term create an obligation for the company to keep that person on in tough times? Does the company's long-term employment create an implied commitment that should constrain the options during a downturn? It is often this concern for commitment and implied promise, rather than fairness, that motivates decisions intended to protect employees or to minimize the impact of layoffs through severance pay and outplacement services.

Similar concerns surface in customer and supplier relations. Carol Williams's decision about Thompson Metals may be determined by the meaning of commitment rather than by a specific concern about fairness. A marketing manager often responds most quickly to long-term customers with whom the manager feels some mutual commitment. Is it appropriate to treat them differently because of such commitment? Are payments beyond stated warranty commitments justified in some cases because of a stronger implied commitment? When a long-term supplier helps to develop a new product but fails to offer the lowest bid for production, does the relationship count for anything? These are the sorts of questions of ethics that arise naturally within management decisions where commitments are believed to be important.

A final principle that is very often the critical concern for thoughtful managers is the injunction to avoid harm. The most direct example, of course, is the physical harm and environmental impact that can result from unsafe workplaces, hazardous products, and the like. It might seem that such examples belong in the first category, where the obligation is clear and implementation is the issue. Some cases may be this straightforward, for instance, when a workplace is so clearly dangerous (e.g., employees work with radioactive materials) that the obligation and the corrective measures (e.g., provide special equipment and procedures) are clear. However, many cases that puzzle us are more complex. What avoiding harm means in a particular instance can be genuinely perplexing.

This is often the case in both workplace and environmental settings when the harmful impact of a product is not yet clear. Should a plant spend large sums to reduce worker exposure to a product when the benefits of doing so are unclear? How much risk is "acceptable"? Who should decide? In the environmental area, the carcinogenic risks of engine emissions are not entirely clear, but the trade-off between emissions regulations and fuel economy is. What is the company or industry obliged to do to avoid harm? How far should it go? What is the role of government regulations in such matters?

While these examples concern undetermined hazards of material products, the impulse to avoid harm extends to other impacts of company action as well. A facilities manager responsible for a new office building ponders the extent of the company's obligation to compensate the residents and businesses displaced by the building, whereeas the chief executive officer considers the overall impact of the company on the community and wonders whether the firm has done enough. A financial analyst "running the numbers" for a new investment in a repressive Latin American country is concerned that the company might be assisting the regime in its repression. And a marketing person in a defense sales area raises new questions about the impact of the company's product and whether the commitment to avoid harm should limit military sales in any way. In all these cases, thoughtful managers are genuinely concerned about the meaning and implications of the moral principle to avoid harm. No one from outside has to beat them over the head with prophetic critique; the very nature of their business activities leads them to ask the questions.

A further complication regarding these considerations of harm arises when the harm, if any, will be directly caused by someone "downstream" from the manager's own company. People of conscience in business will often query whether they or their company should take the initiative to prevent possible harm done by suppliers or customers with whom they have a relationship. If the customer plans to do something with the product that the company would not do (for instance, sell equipment to a repressive regime or mislead the end user about product capacity), what is the company's appropriate—or morally obligatory—action? What if a purchasing agent happens to learn of unethical behavior by a supplier? Is that the purchasing agent's business or not? These are questions of role responsibility directly associated with the concern to avoid harm. They are often very real questions of ethics for managers in the course of their daily rounds.

3. Competing Claims

In the preceding examples, managers worry about the meaning of a particular principle or relationship. Other factors are less salient because the single principle they are concerned about—fairness, honesty, commitment, avoiding harm—is seen to be the critical ethical constraint. But in other cases, more than one principle or relationship is at issue, and competing claims must be carefully judged and integrated or balanced off against one another. All companies have several constituencies, each with distinctive— and sometimes conflicting—interests, and a manager may also find certain commitments in apparent conflict with avoiding harm or being fair. There is no way to categorize such cases easily, but a few examples illustrate how competing claims, too, are questions of ethics that emerge naturally in managerial decisions.

Major corporate policy decisions are the most familiar examples. Should a particular company close its operations in South Africa? Responsible managers will consider the numerous constituencies affected, including South African black employees, the larger South African community, employees and stockholders back home, and U.S. foreign policymakers. They will want to assess what harm is being done by staying versus leaving, what sorts of commitments the company has made to its local workers and the community, and what fairness means in assessing the treatment of black South African employees. Whatever the decision, the process entails considering the many possibly competing claims to a manager's sense of moral obligation.

Selecting sites for new plants or closing existing ones raises similarly diverse sets of claims. Workers and community concerns in each plant site sometimes compete directly with each other for the company's resources; customers, suppliers, and stockholders all have related but distinct interests in the viability of plant sites. Issues of commitment, fairness, honesty, and avoiding harm are all typically at stake, and it is not necessarily clear how these should bear on the final decision.

A well-known example of competing claims arising from business considerations is the crisis faced by Johnson and Johnson when at least one bottle of its Tylenol capsules was tainted with cyanide (apparently by someone intent on harm) in Chicago. The company decided to withdraw the product nationwide until the problem was identified and new, tamper-proof bottles were introduced.[4] One can imagine the multiple claims facing the management as it made this costly decision, including the concern to avoid harm, fairness to its distributors and employees affected by the recall, obligations to shareholders for fiscally responsible decisions, and so on. Company president David Clare captures but one dimension of the experience of competing claims in commenting on the risk of encouraging "terrorists" to use the product to gain attention.

> Should we reintroduce it and . . . risk its happening again? Now, once it had been demonstrated that this was a way to kill people, should we present that opportunity to sick people, or, alternatively, should we go back on because if you don't, then you're giving in to terrorism? What is the balance?[5]

Competing claims arise not only in managing the basic business decisions concerning product, investment, and the like, but also when companies aim to act with "social responsibility" in the public arena through corporate contributions and volunteer services. How much money should be allocated to philanthropy, and how else might those resources be used by the company? Who should benefit from the company's contributions and by what criteria? All sorts of choices must be made in favor of certain groups instead of others, honoring certain commitments and values more than others. The managers of corporate contributions find their jobs virtually defined by the management of competing claims.

Although these policy-level decisions are the most obvious example of the experience of competing claims, it is important to note that individual managers can experience the same questions of ethics in daily management tasks. The distinction between single principle and competing claims issues is a subtle one, for in the former cases there are often competing claims in the background that are simply not major considerations in the problem at hand. Sometimes, these multiple claims do come more fully to the surface in the manager's thinking.

Former Cummins Engine vice-president Charles Powers tells the story of a plant manager pressured to rush the building of a product ahead of a regulatory deadline because the research department had failed to achieve new designs capable of meeting the new regulation.[6] One might see this as simply a legal question, for such early building was clearly legal. The plant manager, however, saw the issue in the more complex terms of competing claims. To be sure, there were strong reasons to build ahead to meet customer demand without regulatory penalties, but he also recognized claims in behalf of the public interest about the safety of the product and the longer-term impact on the company of such activity. He experienced the problem as a set of competing claims to be balanced, rather than one of discerning the meaning of a single principle. (In the end, the plant manager successfully resisted pressures to build before the regulatory deadline.)

Decisions, Decisions: Ethics in Management

As a business manager, then, you can discover different sorts of ethical problems when you ask why you are bothered about a specific dilemma. But these concerns arise in your particular managerial role, not in the vacuum of philosophical analysis. Having defined the nature of the problem more clearly, you then seek to resolve the question within your busy and complex daily work world. That world has several important characteristics affecting your ability to act responsibly.

The Manager's World

The first characteristics are complexity and ambiguity. The company "stands behind its products," but does that mean Smith should offer a settlement beyond warranty requirements in this case? What are the financial implications? Is it fair to other customers? Or another company explicitly prohibits bribery. Does that mean Carlson loses a major order because some goods with papers in legal order cannot get across a border without an "expediting" payment? Even with a stated company policy, a manager faces uncertainty in interpreting the policy in particular cases.

This is nothing new. The purpose of managers with good judgment is to move from overall corporate objectives and policies to particular decisions and actions. Ability to work with complexity and to accept ambiguity often separates a successful, rising manager from one who plateaus at a particular level of responsibility. It is appropriate for an ethicist or a senior manager to articulate a principle, such as being honest with customers, and to acknowledge that tough cases will arise. The manager who has to decide what, exactly, to tell today's customer right now lives with those tough cases. She is the "practitioner" of ethics, for good or ill.

Donald Schön, scholar and experienced management consultant, underscores the importance of this observation with his account of how professionals connect theoretical resources to actual practice.[7] He argues that the typical image of the professional (he includes management in his sense of the term) "applying" theory to "cases" misconstrues reality. Instead, Schön suggests, professionals engage in a "reflective conversation" with unique situations as they discern the appropriate action. From education and experience, a person brings a repertoire of skills, models, and perspectives into rigorous interaction with unique problems and thereby discovers new directions. Schön's model fits well the lived reality of managers who cope daily with complexity and ambiguity. Their ethical decisions come not from application of moral absolutes, but from the interplay of values, concepts, experience, and immediate realities.

A second feature of the manager's world is that decisions typically involve a constant flow of several interrelated decision processes. The elements involved in planning a production run; developing a marketing and sales strategy for a particular customer; purchasing goods and services needed to meet a production schedule; assessing the social-political climate for a foreign investment; or training, developing, and deploying personnel do not hold still. Events unfold, opportunities become contingent on other opportunities and actors, one decision closes off some options and opens others.

What degree of product information and counterargument against a competitor's product is ethically responsible, for instance, when the customer changes strategy during the negotiations and the competitor presents a new marketing angle? Certainly, many actions are simply unethical regardless of circumstances, and many positive responsible actions are generally applicable; but the puzzling areas between these options are broad and stem, in part, from the interrelatedness of so many decisions.

Managers are also faced with the sheer rapidity of the decision process and the necessity to act. Individual managers typically handle this complexity with quick decisions. There are simply too many simultaneous issues and demands on their time to allow for deliberative consideration in every case. Indeed, a critical skill for managers is knowing when to stop the process for careful deliberation; it cannot be stopped every time. The manager who slows down the process too often will in many cases miss the opportunity to decide and will ultimately fail to carry out the managerial task.

Practically, this necessity to act rapidly means deciding what fair treatment to a customer or supplier means in a quick telephone discussion while another call is on hold and two people are waiting at the door with other important issues to discuss. Or it means determining responsible business conduct in the midst of a complex negotiating session in another country where delay may mean losing the business. And, most of all, for many middle managers it means dealing with these and other issues in the midst of a schedule and range of decisions that simply, humanly, do not allow for slow deliberation for anything but the exceptional issue.

A third characteristic of the manager's world is that individual managers assume responsibility for their decisions and actions. Stereotypes of bureaucratic buck-passing notwithstanding, businesspersons typically recognize their own accountability within the system and accept responsibility for their actions. They do so not only in terms of management authority and organizational accountability, but also in the broader sense of personal integrity and moral responsibility for personal choices made in the managerial role. To be sure, there are many opportunities and temptations to avoid responsibility for decisions on the theory that corporate policy or circumstances allow no other choice. Managers are human and susceptible to these excuses and rationalizations. But because they are human, they are keenly aware of their own role and responsibility, as the six stories introduced in chapter 1 illustrate.

This sense of accountability can lead to genuine and positive interest in ethical management. It can also lead simply to an uncomfortable conscience and a lingering anxiety beneath the daily flow of decisions. It may even lead to a conscious narrowing of personal responsibility. That is, because I recognize and accept that I am accountable for my actions, I may look for ways to limit that accountability (for instance, by never acting without clear corporate policy or precedent). Any, indeed all, of these reactions might characterize reactions in a given company. The point is that they all flow from the recognition and acceptance of personal accountability, not the denial of it.

This, then, is the world of managers as they make business decisions and confront questions of ethics. Usually well-paid and eager to perform, they have accepted responsibility for managing a rapid flow of complex and often ambiguous decisions across the whole range of corporate activity. How do we encourage and sustain ethical commitment and ethical decision making in this kind of world?

What Is Needed?

Certainly, a basic requisite is simply good management itself. Good management is not sufficient for ethical management ("What's good for General Motors . . ."), but it is clearly essential. Many ethical problems in companies arise from a failure to plan effectively or from an inflexibility unsuited to the flow of managerial decisions described above. Poor decisions now may eliminate options or pose unacceptable trade-offs down the road that could have been avoided with better management in the first place.

Examples abound at all organizational levels. A foreman refuses to listen to an employee's suggestion about machine maintenance. Later, he faces the difficult choice of shipping defective parts or putting himself at risk with higher-level management for failing to meet production goals. A plant manager chooses to postpone retooling the line because of short-term pressures and ends up with the same pressures and choices the first-line supervisor faced. And a senior officer fails to recognize the need for product-line changes until the competition is a jump ahead. Suddenly, the senior officer is pressuring the plant for rapid changes that may generate just the sort of problems the plant manager and first-line supervisor are already facing. In these cases and many others, good management may prevent an ethical dilemma from arising. Likewise, sound management considerations will often be consistent with ethical duties, as in treating employees with respect and being a trustworthy supplier.

Management is best when it is anticipatory and affirmative, coordinating resources to meet changing circumstances, anticipating possible competing claims and ethical duties while there is still time for choice. Questions of ethics arise even in well-managed organizations. Ethical issues will become even more difficult in those that are poorly managed.

Closely linked to anticipatory management is creative moral imagination, the capacity to recognize ethical issues, to rise above too restricted a horizon in assessing an issue, to see the stakes involved for those affected, and to generate alternatives.[8] Often, managers at any level simply fail to see the ethical dimension of a decision or to see it too narrowly. Evelyn and Carol have counterparts who might not even raise the questions they see as obvious ones. Another manager in their shoes might define the issue so narrowly as to miss creative possibilities and multiple alternatives. One could imagine Carol making a preemptive, absolutist judgment that she cannot reduce orders to Thompson Metals in a way that virtually paralyzes her in her managerial role. Her solution might or might not turn out to be a responsible one, but failure to consider alternatives imaginatively could well heighten her stress and diminish her ability to make a responsible decision.

In cases of single principle/single relationship and competing claims issues, managers also need conceptual tools to analyze ethical dimensions of business decisions. Just as we have concepts and rules of thumb to assess return on investment, market target volumes, and factory inventory levels, so we need help in knowing whether fairness is the right category for a particular decision or whether a questionable payment really is a bribe. Managers, especially top and middle management, need familiarity with these concepts to bring them to bear confidently in their dynamic world. This is especially true, since most managers receive little or no instruction concerning such concepts in their education and preparation for business careers.

Managers also need the ability to articulate their ethical reasoning so that they can explain and defend their decisions, on occasion, to peers and supervisors; to the public, perhaps; and, most importantly, to themselves. The increasing attention to questions of ethics in business lies behind the importance of articulating reasons within the company and to the public. In addition, our own sense of accountability and responsibility moves us to understand ethics better, so that we gain more confidence that we are, indeed, exercising our role responsibly. That confidence comes finally from a sense of personal integrity and the ability to convince ourselves of the rightness of our actions. Here, again, practical analytic concepts become important.

Recognition and analytic concepts are critical features of ethical decision making in management. But, as we see by recalling Schön's characterization of professional practice, managerial judgment also requires the capacity to resolve issues, to take the leap from analysis to integrated judgment. Anyone trained in financial analysis, for instance, can "run the numbers" on a proposed deal or compare two or three capital investments; but the difference between a fresh MBA graduate and a seasoned veteran is that ability to move beyond the analytic resources and discern when to close the negotiations or which investment is the best combination of risk and return. The analytic tools become part of the repertoire that reflective managers combine with experience, insight, and response to the peculiar circumstances of a particular deal as they reach a final judgment. So it is with questions of ethics as well. Managers at every level need not only the ability to sort out competing claims and to understand such terms as fairness or honesty, but also the capacity, which comes only with practice, to integrate these considerations into a responsible judgment that is faithful to ethical principles, to role responsibility, and to personal integrity.

What we need, then, to enable effective and ethical business performance is dynamic, anticipatory management, enriched by moral imagination and the capacities to assess and to resolve questions of ethics within the complex flow of daily decision making. The framework in the following chapters offers some practical tools and perspectives for this ongoing task.

CHAPTER THREE

Who Else Matters?
Responsibility To Stakeholders

As Sun Ship wound down its business, the managers devoted substantial time, energy, and emotional resources to working with employees and community representatives to ease the impact of the company's decline. Large sums of money were also provided, not only to employees through severance pay but also to the community for various purposes. Why should Sun Ship spend its resources in this way? Why not pay only what was legally required to employees and to local taxing authorities, thus minimizing the cost to Sun Ship and maximizing the resources available for the parent company's use elsewhere?

The answer lies in management's recognition of competing claims from legitimate "stakeholders," from persons and groups who had a "stake" in the company's actions. Steve Simpson and his colleagues asked themselves, "Who else matters in carrying out the difficult task of winding down the shipyard business?" Implicitly, they were applying the traditional Golden Rule, "Do unto others as you would have them do unto you," by considering the impact on others. Managers can apply the same considerations in their own cases by considering their circles of responsibility to various stakeholders.

Circles of Responsibility: Respect for Stakeholders

The Golden Rule articulates a simple reciprocity in human relations that says we should consider the impact of our actions on others as if we were on the receiving end. This is no more than simple recognition of our common humanity and the fundamental ground of ethics in respect for persons. This familiar and traditional ethic in interpersonal relations applies equally well to corporations and to the managers who make decisions on their behalf. In the corporate context, we embody this concern by attending to responsibility toward stakeholders. Stakeholders are persons, groups, and organizations that have a stake in the activities of the company. They are the ones who are directly affected, for good or for ill, by corporate action. They include stockholders, to be sure, but employees, customers, suppliers, local communities, host countries, and government agencies are also stakeholders.

Just as individuals attend to the impact of their actions on others, so the company looks to the effects of its action on these various stakeholders. Asking who else matters in resolving ethical questions in management means identifying the affected stakeholders and considering what interests they may have, what commitments have been made to them, and what impact proposed actions may have on them.

The underlying philosophy is that business corporations hold a kind of public trust. Society requires business enterprise for human well-being, and individual corporations derive their power ultimately from society's consent that the business is fulfilling its public trust. Managers are not simply responsible to "owners" but also to the wider community that needs the industry and whose support is

Figure 1. Stakeholders

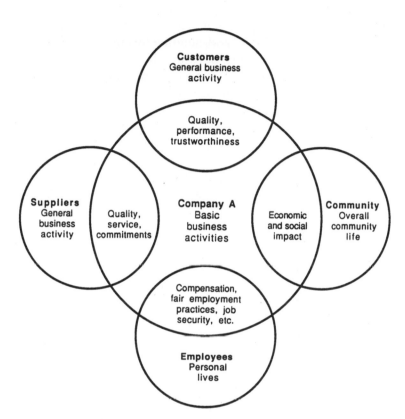

necessary for successful operation. Recognizing responsibility to stakeholders is a step in this direction.

The circle diagram in figure 1 will help to illustrate the point. The company's primary activity is defined by the large center circle. Within this arena, managers carry on the whole range of normal business activities necessary to fulfill the company's social role in the economy. For example, financial services companies develop and deliver insurance and investment products, and manufacturing firms produce and distribute tangible goods. In the design of our political economy, private businesses serve the larger needs of society by these production and distribution activities. General Motors makes cars, Aetna provides insurance, Kellogg produces breakfast cereal. These tasks define the fundamental identity and business activity of each company, represented by the large center circle. A critical ethical obligation of the firm is to fulfill this basic business activity as effectively as possible because of its place in the larger scheme of things. It is, of course, possible to make ethical judgments about the company's basic activity as well, as in debates over tobacco or nerve gas production.

As they go about this business, however, managers discover that the company's activities inevitably overlap with the interests and activities of various stakeholders (to keep the drawing simple, figure 1 illustrates only a few stakeholders). These areas of overlap constitute the primary focus of responsibility to stakeholders. In the course of doing business, the company affects employees and must attend to issues of safety, fairness, and commitment. It has a direct impact on customers in such areas as quality, service, and trustworthiness. It receives capital from shareholders, who are owed responsible business practices leading to financial return. It gains benefits from and in turn directly impacts the community in many ways. Responsibility to stakeholders means that managers attend to the interests of the stakeholders relevant to a particular decision. They must ask, "Who else matters?"

But the company is not responsible for every interest of

its stakeholders. The circles overlap, but they remain distinct. There are many interests in the community and in the lives of employees for which the company is not responsible and, indeed, arenas that are none of the company's business. Not every community problem is the responsibility even of a large and socially responsible firm, and the company has no business intervening in its employees' personal lives (by, for instance, pressuring employees to vote in certain ways). There may be good reasons for a company to extend into the outer circles in particular circumstances, but these activities will always be limited. The task of the responsible manager, then, is both to identify the relevant stakeholders and to distinguish between legitimate interests within the company's circle and less clear claims that may arise from outside.

What about day care for the children of employees, for example? In the past, this responsibility has been clearly within the employee's personal circle, well outside the company's. But as more couples begin a family while both parents work and as the need for day care outstrips the supply in many communities, corporations are often asked to help. Is day care legitimately within the company's circle? Reasonable people might argue both sides, although it is likely that over the next several years, day care will move into the employer's circle as a customary activity.

Consider again Steve Simpson's decisions about closing Sun Ship. In this case the company tried to sustain its basic circle of activity (and thereby to continue to contribute jobs and taxes to the community and financial return to shareholders) in the face of business pressures to which it finally succumbed. As Simpson assessed what Sun Company needed to do for employees and the community, he clearly accepted the notion that Sun Ship's closing would hurt stakeholders "inside the circle." Severance pay for workers and financial assistance to the community are inside the overlapping circles of responsibility as integral to the impact of this final business decision of Sun Ship. Such payments are not mere generosity or sentimental gestures.

Steve Simpson also experienced the competing claims of different stakeholder interests. Steve steadfastly kept to himself the dollar amount his company was willing to commit to the closing process. He understood the potential conflict between the financial interests of Sun Ship's shareholders and the claims of employees and communities. Furthermore, many in the community made claims for assistance that Steve interpreted as going outside Sun Ship's circle of responsibility. That many community and labor people generally praised the benefits Sun Ship provided suggests that Steve did a good job of balancing these competing claims.

We can see how this same framework would help some of our other managers assess their questions of ethics. Wendell Johnson is struggling with the limits of his responsibility to Mac, the employee with a poor performance record. By asking who else matters, he will be reminded of his responsibilities to other employees and to customers and shareholders in assessing Mac's performance fairly and accurately. Likewise, Carol Williams will recognize the important interests of customers, other suppliers, and stockholders as she decides how to respond to Mel Thompson's appeal for special treatment. But Wendell and Carol focus their attention on Mac and Mel because they see them as the most important and immediately affected stakeholders. Here the overlapping circles remind them of the limits to their responsibility. Wendell must be fair to Mac, but he is not responsible for all of Mac's personal problems. Carol wants to honor the loyalty represented by the overlap of her company's circle with Thompson Metals's, but she is not responsible for all of Thompson's problems. The framework in the next chapter will help to sort out these issues, but the circle chart already helps to focus the issues.

Obviously, one cannot stop every decision process to pull out this chart and develop a checklist of stakeholders. But the framework does help when time for reflection is short. Even if a manager is in the midst of frantic activity, familiarity with the notion of stakeholders can inform the quick judgments that are often necessary.

Profits and Justice: Corporations in Society

Profits

But what about the traditional free enterprise explanation of business behavior that leaves only a small realm for managerial ethics: honesty, integrity, and other simple virtues of personal behavior? In this view most issues, including the closing of a company, are handled by the market rather than by individual managerial choice. Moreover, individuals who try to make "responsible" choices will simply undercut their goals by thwarting the efficiency of the market. Dynamic market exchange is deemed the most effective and responsible way to determine all sorts of questions—what products deserve to be on the market, whether a plant should close down, how to protect employee rights in the corporation, and many others. This viewpoint, most notably defended by Nobel Prize–winner Milton Friedman, holds that managers are agents of owners and should play their role in the market by representing only the owners' interests. The title of Friedman's famous essay, "The Social Responsibility of Business Is to Increase Its Profits,"[1] summarizes his view.

This dominant model, even ideology, of a "free market" economy leads many businesspeople to skepticism about ethics in business management. But the realities of the contemporary corporate world increasingly pose problems that the market model does not fit. Ever larger and more complex corporate organizations distance managers from the shareholders, whose profit-making agents they are supposed to be. Meanwhile, many shareholders invest in stocks for overall liquidity and financial return, and they are not interested in careful monitoring and control of management. Managers thus have more discretionary power than the traditional market model allows. We have already seen how questions of ethics emerge as part of the very process of management in this environment. Simultaneously, a host of decisions made by managers seems to fall outside the presumed efficient responsibility of market mechanisms. Certainly, a company's advocacy of public policies and political candidates is not subject to significant market restraints. Nor does the market protect members of a local community when a large company moves or goes out of business. And the discretion of corporations to respect or mistreat employees, suppliers, and customers is, in many cases, almost immune from market discipline (at least in the short to medium term).[2]

In these and many similar instances, the traditional market model is inadequate. Certainly, market discipline plays a central role in the way our overall economic system functions. Competition in the marketplace does govern much corporate activity. But to say that managers should simply maximize profits as agents of shareholders assumes that the market dynamics are always effective and relatively quick to respond. If so, it is possible that competitive pressures would prevent the worst abuses. The truth, however, is that this assumption is invalid for a whole range of corporate decisions. And when the assumption is false, the injunction becomes dangerous. If managers are ignoring realms of corporate impact removed from market constraints, immense injury can occur to employees, customers, communities, and the public interest. This reality gives rise to the notion of responsibility to stakeholders.

Justice

While some are skeptical of corporate ethics because of their devotion to free market ideology, others share this skepticism because they see irreconcilable conflicts between social justice and contemporary economic structures. Citizen action coalitions, political groups, and religious organizations are often among those criticizing the justice of specific business decisions and of the economic system in general. Their critique, which is part of the manager's social environment, raises concerns for the poor and disadvantaged, for more just distribution of resources, and for more participatory structures in economic and political life.

Evelyn Bates could well ask herself whether Omega office products serve the poor and whether her compensation package as an officer of the company is just. Wendell might wonder whether more democratic corporate decision making is an important goal in his circumstances. Meanwhile, Charles Warren himself appears to be a victim of the lack of more humane and just corporate policies and procedures.

People like Charles Warren are victimized because the corporate structure and ethos of his company are oriented to a narrow definition of gain. The people at the bottom are often viewed as replaceable and expendable, their human dignity ignored. Corporate emphasis on production goals, marketing efforts, and profitability can lead to such problems as unsafe products, environmental pollution, and economic hardship and uncertainty in plant communities facing a shutdown.

At the systemic level, the power and impact of large corporations on our political and cultural life is immense. In concluding his study of politics and markets, with its sharp critique of the modern business corporation, Charles Lindblom wonders aloud at the contradictions between "big business" and democracy, such as disproportionate resources in private hands and opportunities to make or break communities. He concludes: "The large private corporation fits oddly into democratic theory and vision. Indeed, it does not fit at all."[3]

The force of such criticisms is important to social policy debates and to personal decisions about participation in the corporate world. But the social justice critique does not help managers in daily decision making. J. Irwin Miller, chair of the Executive Committee of the Board at Cummins Engine Company, makes the point clearly in the story of a manager who cannot get a shipment across the Indonesian border without giving the customs clerk a hundred-dollar bribe. What should a responsible manager do? Caricaturing the response of well-intentioned critics, Miller told a group of future ministers that they might respond like this:

> [You can] tell him that corporate America is a cruel system indeed, that it must be changed in the interest of equity and justice not only for exploited workers, but as well for trapped middle managers like himself. You can even add

that . . . you are going to dedicate your own ministry to working for political, economic and social change. That may hearten him, but what if he goes on to say, "That's great, but what do I tell our employee in Jakarta this afternoon?"[4]

Managers may well agree with many of the critiques of the economic system, or at least agree that various community groups ought to raise such issues, but they live out their responsibilities, in a sense, in the meantime. Whatever the larger social-political reforms needed, managers like Steve Simpson and Carol Williams do their jobs every day. Within the limits of current structures they seek to do so responsibly. Miller comments:

All corporate decisions are tough, and they are tough because, out in the world of organized human endeavor, the decision-maker almost never has the luxury of choosing between right and wrong, instead almost always finds himself or herself forced to choose between two wrongs.[5]

Although the stakeholder concept may not adequately address all the larger social-political issues, it is consistent with the general theme of social justice critiques because attention to a company's circles of responsibility emphasizes its interdependence with society. More important, for individual managers who must make the difficult choices to which Miller refers, the stakeholder notion is a practical tool for responsible decision making. It, along with the other practical questions examined in subsequent chapters, will help people like Evelyn Bates and Wendell Johnson in their day-to-day tasks.

Who, Me? Management as Service

Most corporate policies and decisions are shaped by persons of good conscience operating in what Miller calls "a very murky world indeed."[6] And this murky world is our world. The corporate decisions are real ones that affect the fabric of our daily lives. We rely on the goods and services produced by corporations for the infrastructure of modern living and for most of the artifacts of daily life. Whatever the broader political and economic changes needed, in the meantime women and men in corporate roles have to tell someone in Jakarta what to do countless times every day.

Managers, therefore, provide an indispensable social service. Popular stereotypes of big business and of greedy, deceitful managers mislead us into immediate skepticism about such a claim. But without the day-to-day efforts of business managers, the very fabric of our own daily living would come apart. And without their integrity and sensitivity, the mutual respect so essential to our common life would disintegrate. Profit taken to an extreme can represent blind greed, but profitability as a means and measure for effective, viable commercial activity helps to ensure the distribution of goods and services to stakeholders. Managers contribute to the wider community not only through the more obvious voluntary activities and charitable giving, but even more importantly in their daily work sustaining the economic fabric of the community.

Think, for example, of our six managers in chapter 1 as persons whose positions offer such opportunities for service. Charles is explicit about this and affirms that he seeks to live by consistent values at home and at work. Although his comments illustrate some rationalization and anxiety about his efforts, Charles recognizes that honest business dealings are part of responsible living. Carol Williams's concern for Thompson Metals and Wendell Johnson's efforts to treat Mac fairly are examples of how life in institutions opens possibilities to help other persons. How

Carol deals with Mel and other suppliers, how Wendell deals with Mac and other employees contribute to just and humane common life in the business community.

Steve Simpson has a particularly powerful opportunity to carry the burden of institutional responsibility. The impact of closing a shipyard demonstrates how important responsible management is to the lives of people and communities. In Sharon Metzger's public affairs role and Evelyn Bates's management of Omega's overseas investments, we see the impact that business decisions have for good or for ill in human affairs.

The manager who is preoccupied with delivery or production schedules or with resolving a difficult personnel problem may well respond to these suggestions with surprise. "Who, me?" is a natural reaction in light of the low expectations the public often holds for businesspersons. But it is a simple fact that the day-to-day activities of these managers has significant impact on a variety of stakeholders. The managers who ask "Who else matters?" recognize not only the ethical importance of these relationships but also their opportunity for service to specific stakeholders and to the common good of the whole community.

CHAPTER FOUR

Is It My Problem?
The Practical Meaning of Ethics

Wendell Johnson has made a decision to fire Mac—or has he?

> The issue I'm struggling with at this point is balancing what's the best thing for the employee and what's best for the organization. I think I have made the decision. . . . Anyway, the guilt trip is over. He performs or he's fired. It's simple. Except that it won't be that simple. It's just easy to say.[1]

Wendell has already considered who else matters, and he knows that Mac's performance problem must be addressed for the sake of other employees and the company's external stakeholders. He also knows he has substantial grounds for terminating Mac where their circles of responsibility overlap. Mac owes the company adequate performance, and the company has legitimate expectations for such performance. But Wendell's anxiety about the decision is not merely sentimental reluctance to tell Mac such an unpleasant message. He is also concerned whether the company has fulfilled its end of the bargain. If so, Mac's personal difficulties are not Wendell's problem. They are outside his company's circle of responsibility. However, if the company has not treated Mac fairly in the process, then Wendell has to admit this is his problem, too.

Wendell recounts the many chances Mac has been given and suggests that Mac has no excuse for not knowing his performance weaknesses and areas for improvement. If he is right, he can honestly answer "no" to the question "Is this my problem?" On the other hand, Wendell's own uncertainty about termination and the fact that one personnel unit suggests Mac be given another chance raises the possibility that the company has not been entirely fair to Mac up to this point. Indeed, he might reflect on his own comment that Mac "knows" he'll be fired by July, yet, "I haven't said explicitly that he will be fired July 1." In his own emotional struggle with Mac's case, Wendell may have avoided the difficult but honest communication necessary to give Mac a fair chance at improving. If so, he might conclude that the company does, indeed, share some responsibility, and he might decide that something must first be done to rectify that wrong. Correcting any problems caused by unclear performance feedback must come before considering termination. Indeed, Wendell's story in chapter 1 suggests that he has already endeavored to accomplish such corrective action by working closely with Mac on specific performance problems.

Wendell is wrestling with an important moral insight. He must accept responsibility for problems resulting from his (or the company's) actions, but he is not responsible for all the problems he inevitably encounters. Asking the question "Is this my problem?" is an important discipline in sorting out when and how to respond. Let's see how this simple question can provide a framework building on Wendell's own insight.

Is It My Problem? Obligations and Good Deeds

Consider a personal and then a corporate example.[2] Suppose you encounter a beggar as you walk down the street of a large city. Should you hand over your "spare change"? Should you help the person find shelter or even take a continuing interest in her or his welfare on your return home? The answers are not obvious, for they depend on your understanding of why persons beg, your other charitable commitments and priorities, your financial means, and your current task. Opportunities for good deeds abound, and this may or may not be an appropriate one for you. But if asked whether you should intentionally push the beggar off the chair into the street, surely all responsible persons would say "no." At a minimum, we agree that we should not harm others, whatever our purpose and destination may be as we walk by. And if you accidentally knock the beggar down, breaking her cup, we would probably agree that you owe her a helping hand, an apology, and a new cup. Injury that we cause requires that we compensate the injured.

The same distinction applies in corporate activity. Much of the debate about "corporate social responsibility" focuses on doing good deeds such as contributing to charitable programs, providing extra funds to enhance architectural beauty or employee well-being, or donating executives' time and talent to community groups. These actions may be laudable and can certainly be understood as moral responsibilities rooted in respect for persons in the community. But they represent choices from among a multitude of possible good deeds, choices open to debate depending on the circumstances and on one's view of morality and the role of corporations. In contrast, there are fewer disputes that corporations should not knowingly market unsafe products (the definition of "unsafe," of course, occasions significant debate). Product safety is a moral obligation, not a good deed. In terms of the stakeholder notion represented in the circles of responsibility chart (see figure 1, chapter 3), avoiding injury within the overlapping circles is a minimal moral obligation, like not knocking down the beggar, whereas reaching out to help within a stakeholder's wider circle might be good, but it is not necessarily an obligation.

A first step in determining role responsibility, then, is the simple injunction "Do no harm." At the most basic level, this obligation not to harm others is more stringent than the responsibility to help others by good deeds. Virtually all ethical systems, even in different cultures, acknowledge a moral minimum that prohibits doing injury to others and, as a corollary, requires corrective action when injury is done. The practical meaning for our purposes is the injunction to do no harm to stakeholders in the course of carrying out the company's business activities. But what does this enjoin?

While a precise definition will lead to disagreements about human nature and needs, a reasonably specific range of considerations offers a core definition despite inevitable ambiguities at the edges. The harm that can be done to stakeholders includes the following:

1. material injury, including direct assault; impairment of health; deprivation of food, clothing, and shelter; and economic loss;
2. deprivation of freedom, including political rights and personal choice;
3. violation of moral principles such as promise keeping, honesty, and fairness.

Avoiding harm to stakeholders, then, means attending to all those situations in which the company's circle of activity overlaps those of various stakeholders. Is there possibility of material injury to workers through unsafe working conditions or to customers through faulty equipment that results in financial losses due to delays? Might the company's lobbying efforts impose the power of the employer on individual employees' political choices? Does a proposed merger or buy-out transaction risk betraying commitments to current shareholders or unfair treatment to employees? Where the answer to questions such as these is yes, responsible managers have a moral obligation to try to avoid such injury and, if that proves impossible, to find appropriate ways of compensating the injured.

Because management daily involves a host of stakeholder relationships, this injunction to avoid harm lies at the heart of ethical management. But "avoid," although technically correct, wrongly conveys a notion of passivity. As noted earlier, good management is anticipatory. In this context, anticipatory management means being alert to the ways in which decisions will impact stakeholders and actively seeking to avoid harm as one goes about the managerial task. The lack of such anticipation leads to what Charles Powers calls "head in the hands ethics," that is, the discovery that one is caught in a difficult ethical dilemma with no way out but to bury head in hands with a sigh of despair.[3] The obligation to avoid injury, then, is best understood as proactive acceptance of basic ethical obligations, together with obligations to correct problems that one has caused.

This is the first and most important response to the question "Is it *my* problem?" But these most stringent ethical obligations do not exhaust moral responsibility. Where there are human needs and opportunities for personal and community growth, ethical concern rooted in respect for persons leads also to doing good deeds "above and beyond the call of duty." In management, such good deeds are done when the company reaches out beyond the overlapping area of its own circle with a stakeholder's to provide specific assistance in the stakeholder's arena. Thus, for instance, corporate assistance to renters being displaced by a new company office building is an obligation within the overlapping circles, whereas a corporate gift to help build the new community opera house reaches beyond that immediate relationship into the wider community. But given the variety and limitless opportunities for such good deeds, choices must be made.

A simple example is personal charitable giving. From among the numerous solicitations received each year from worthy organizations, I must choose those to which to devote my limited funds. This choice should not be seen as a negative reflection on the worth of the charities declined. Rather, it represents my limited resources and my particular commitments and interests. So it is with the full range of possible good deeds. We choose, from among a multitude of potential projects, limited patterns of commitment that express our own moral sensitivities and unique identities.

The same dynamic occurs in corporate settings. Like individuals, firms have limited resources and distinctive identities that are reflected in their commitments to corporate good deeds. More than individuals, firms must limit these commitments. Business organizations, after all, have already accepted a socially defined role to accomplish good through their particular product or service. Good deeds, if vigorously pursued, could pull the company away from its primary task and exhaust its resources. But some effort beyond its own circle is appropriate to give expression to the company's citizenship and participation in the wider community. The amount and nature of corporate charitable contributions, special fringe benefits to employees, and corporate championing of particular social causes illustrate the variety of such commitments.

Doing good deeds is an important but limited activity of business corporations. The injunction to avoid harm in the basic business arena comes first. No amount of charitable good deeds, such as support for the symphony or contributions to economic development agencies, will "make up" for harm done in the course of doing business, such as polluting local waterways, maintaining unsafe workplaces, or treating customers and suppliers unfairly.

Kew Gardens Principle

Thus far, the framework I am suggesting builds on Wendell's own insights about the nature and extent of his obligations to Mac. If he and his colleagues have not been fair to Mac, then they owe Mac further steps before terminating him. But if they have proactively anticipated their obligations and have treated Mac well, then it might seem to be only a voluntary good deed (and perhaps an ill-advised one at that) if Wendell tries to give Mac still another chance. But suppose that in the conversation about termination, Mac appeals to Wendell for another chance on the grounds that his wife is ill, Mac needs ten more months to qualify for the pension plan, and he has nowhere else to turn for employment. If Wendell has handled the case properly, he can certainly recognize that this is Mac's problem, not his own. But, feeling Mac's pain and his own empathy for Mac's hard times, he might well ask himself, "Can I just ignore all this? Is he in such dire straits that I really ought to help him?"

This concern represents another kind of ethical question that does not fit neatly into the two categories we have considered so far. Such cases occur when, although we have not done any harm to another, offering aid seems more than mere generosity, given the other's clear need. Consider again the beggar. If she were lying on the curb, a bloodied victim of an accident, we would certainly take notice. And if no one else seemed to be coming to her aid, we might well feel an obligation to help her rather than simply pass by.

What is at stake here is, again, role responsibility. There is clearly a problem, but is it our problem? A set of considerations collectively known as the Kew Gardens Principle helps to decide the matter in such cases.[4] It takes its name from a tragic murder in the Kew Gardens section of New York City many years ago, a murder witnessed by thirty to forty bystanders, none of whom so much as screamed to alarm the assailant or called police to come to the victim's aid. Surely, this is an obvious case when we would ordinarily believe that helping another is an essential moral responsibility. The Kew Gardens Principle identifies characteristics of this obvious case that can be applied to more puzzling circumstances.

The more that each of four factors applies when you face a question of helping with a problem you did not cause, the greater is your responsibility to act. The four elements of the Kew Gardens Principle are:

1. Need   There is a clear problem that must be resolved; the greater the need, the greater the responsibility to act if the other three factors are applicable.

2. Proximity   You are "close" to the situation, not necessarily in space but certainly in terms of notice; you know of the need or

could reasonably be held responsible for
knowing of it.

3. Capability   You have some means by which to aid
the one in need without undue risk.

4. Last Resort No one else is likely to help. The first
three factors create an assumption to aid
the one in need. This assumption is
strengthened to the degree that you are
likely to be the only one who will, in fact,
help. Given our propensity to fail to act
on the false assumption that others will
do so, the burden of proof here is in favor
of acting.

Obviously, this principle works clearly in interpersonal
settings of dire need. The original case in Kew Gardens,
New York, involved danger to life (need), admitted awareness of the incident (proximity), opportunity to frighten the
assailant or telephone police (capacity), and a reasonable
possibility—in the event, a reality—that others might not
act (last resort). Since we know the beggar's plight if she is
lying in the street (need and proximity), and we have the
capability to hail a police officer or call an ambulance, our
judgment in that case depends on whether others seem
likely to help. Without any sign of such help, it would be
irresponsible to pass by.

The principle is also applicable in managerial decisions
as a helpful tool, particularly in questions of ethics that
seem to be on the margins of the circles of responsibility.
For example, what if Wendell applied the Kew Gardens
principle in the hypothetical development we just considered? Clearly, there is a need; Mac will be out a job, with all
the implications that has for him and his family. And

Wendell is painfully proximate; Mac sits across the desk looking defeated and in despair.

What about capability? That depends on circumstances in the company at the time. If this is a tight year and the company has relatively few employees to begin with, there may simply be no room to maneuver in assisting Mac. On the other hand, in a large company in a good year, it is possible there are other tasks Mac might be assigned until he is vested in the pension. Wendell needs to consider here, however, not only financial capability but also the impact on other workers who might see this as unfair treatment or as a precedent committing the company to similar actions in the future. One can imagine Wendell concluding either way on the capability issue.

If he does see some capacity for acting, Wendell must then consider whether he—more accurately, the company—is the last resort in helping Mac. In general, the answer is clearly no. Mac is a mature adult who ought to be responsible for his own life. Nevertheless, Wendell might conclude, as he listens to the whole story, that Mac really is without any other alternatives. In that case, depending on the need and the capacity of the company, Wendell might conceivably offer Mac some special assistance, ranging from extra job counseling and extended benefits to continued employment in some fashion.

I am not suggesting that this conclusion is inevitable using the Kew Gardens Principle. Rather, the principle provides Wendell with some points of reference for thinking more clearly about his obligations. What conclusion he reaches will be shaped by complicated answers to the questions, particularly the capability and last resort questions. The principle, as well as the overall framework of obligations and good deeds, helps managers like Wendell not only to respond to important obligations, but also to understand when there are legitimate limits to their responsibilities. Using Kew Gardens, Wendell might well conclude responsibly that Mac's problems are beyond Wendell's managerial role, no matter how concerned he might be personally with Mac's dilemma.

Suppose a community group pressures a company to provide remedial job training, using its corporate training facilities to help a community-based program work with the so-called structurally unemployed. Such an enterprise might be justified as a good and generous corporate program, an opportunity for doing a good deed if the company chooses to do so. But the community group argues that the company has a stronger ethical obligation. It must, they say, provide this help as part of its role in the community. As executives consider the issue, the Kew Gardens Principle might help them to agree with the community group or to understand better why they disagree. The community need is clearly documented, and the company knows about it, so the assessment would turn primarily on capability and last resort. The company has training capabilities, to be sure, but its financial constraints and business needs for the training facility would affect the assessment of capability. Responsible managers would also look at the last resort question, inquiring whether other firms and agencies are responding to the need and how the company's own involvement might fit into the community-wide resources for such training. Disagreements in this assessment are sure to arise, but the principle does provide a framework for assessing the issues.

Together with the distinction between moral obligations and good deeds, the Kew Gardens Principle provides a helpful approach to assessing role responsibility. You can assess your managerial role responsibility across a range of choices. "Is it my problem?" Where you and your company have actually caused injury, the answer is yes. You have the most stringent moral obligation to compensate in some fashion. Good deeds to the community should not take resources away from fulfilling this obligation. Day to day, your most fundamental obligation is to carry out your managerial tasks while maintaining obligations to stakeholders. This is the arena in which many of the questions of ethics discussed earlier most typically arise. Even if you conclude that the company has met its basic ethical obligations, the Kew Gardens Principle may occasionally suggest some obligation to act. And, finally, within limitations, you may conclude that a good deed is in order.

What Is the Ethical Concern?
The Practical Meaning of Ethical Principles

In struggling with the question of his responsibility to Mac, Wendell is implicitly trying to "locate" the issue along this continuum of ethical responsibilities. Does he owe corrective action? Has he handled the obligations proactively? Is there a Kew Gardens obligation? But locating the issue (it is my problem or perhaps it is not), while important, is an incomplete step. Once you discern your role responsibility—that is, decide that the problem is legitimately yours to solve—you must then identify the relevant principle and assess its meaning for the problem at hand. Wendell, for instance, is clearly concerned with the practical meaning of fairness in the way Mac has been treated. Other typical principles that arise in business decisions include keeping promises and commitments, dealing honestly, accomplishing good and avoiding or preventing harm, and complying with the law. Analysis of the practical meaning of these principles is always specific to particular circumstances, so I will illustrate the process with the questions raised by Wendell, Carol Williams, and Evelyn Bates.

Fairness to Mac

Wendell wants to be fair to Mac. But what does fairness mean? We can probably agree that the essence of fair treatment is treating people equally when there are no relevant differences between them. On that we typically agree. The challenge lies in deciding which categories are relevant, and which are not, for differential treatment. In distributing the right to vote, for instance, we say that only a few differences are relevant, such as age and legal status. But when we provide salary and promotions, we do not use the same standard. It would be unfair, we say, to pay everyone the same. Relevant differences in compensation include such job-related factors as contribution and productivity. Productivity is irrelevant to voting ability in a democracy, but it may be very germane to who shares in profits generated by productive labor. In both examples, voting rights and compensation, we determine what are relevant differences by looking to the nature of the good that is being distributed. In Michael Walzer's felicitous phrase, we look to the particular sphere of justice, to the particular relationships and goods that are at stake in a particular distribution.[5]

Thus, for instance, if a compensation system provides profit-linked bonuses for higher-level managers, on the theory that their performance more directly affects profits than does that of lower-level employees, then the same difference is relevant when profits are down and salaries must be cut—the higher-level managers ought to bear a larger burden. Better yet, perhaps the company begins to assess its assumption and determines that all employees contribute sufficiently to profitability, that there are no relevant differences apart from those already reflected in basic salary scales. Then, as many companies are doing, it might develop a profit-sharing system for all employees.

For Wendell, the question is what counts as fair treatment in performance evaluation and termination. Jobs are provided to achieve the goals of the organization. In Wendell's department, the tasks concern quality service to customers when products pose problems in the field. Factors relevant for fair performance evaluation would be specific accomplishments and failures measured against specific objectives for successful activities in the field. Irrelevant factors include being the son-in-law of the boss, having technical skill and training in something entirely unrelated to job performance, or having political and personal opinions that differ from the supervisor. It would be unfair for such characteristics to affect performance evaluation because they are unrelated to ability to perform the job.

Wendell is clear that Mac has failed on objective, job-related performance characteristics. There is little doubt from what he says that Mac could be terminated fairly in light of his performance failures. Are there differences in his case that are relevant to different treatment, however? We have examined some possibilities in the earlier discussion of Wendell's problem. If Mac has not been told of his deficiencies then it would, indeed, be unfair to terminate him without first communicating the weaknesses and seeing whether he could improve. Mac's personal problems raise another possible difficulty. Is it unfair to terminate someone with a sick wife, no pension, and little prospect for other employment? Here Wendell must be careful about the meaning of fairness and his own managerial role.

There are at least two possible answers to the question. One is to recognize that the job is related to performance, not to problems and issues in the employee's personal life. These are irrelevant to the job, and it is therefore fair to proceed with the termination. Indeed, to provide special treatment opens up other problems of fairness, for how will the company decide which personal problems are relevant and which are not in its diverse work force? Making an exception for Mac may be unfair to the others. None of this discounts the pain of Mac's situation or Wendell's human anguish in confronting Mac, but it does help Wendell to understand that in his management role, he can terminate someone like Mac without being unfair.

Another possible interpretation of fairness here is to argue that Mac's problem is, indeed, a relevant difference justifying differential treatment. While not directly related to the job itself, Mac's personal circumstances are relevant to how the company is perceived to treat people and whether it has a reputation as a compassionate employer. Wendell might then argue that the company should terminate persons with weak performance except under certain circumstances, such as when an employee is at a given age and a specified period of time short of being vested in the pension fund. While it is possible to follow this interpretation, the implications would need to be addressed carefully because of the difficulty of narrowly defining the exceptional conditions.

I suggest two interpretations because reasonable people can disagree about what constitute relevant differences. Clear thinking about fairness will not magically yield agreeable solutions every time. But the process of thinking carefully about fairness and relevant differences can contribute to a more thoughtful resolution of confusions and conflicts about management responsibility.

Commitment to Thompson Metals

Carol Williams has a problem with the implications of commitment to Thompson Metals over the years. Presumably any explicit promises and contractual arrangements have been fulfilled. If not, Carol would be obliged to insist that her company compensate Thompson for the financial losses incurred as a result of the company's failure to live up to its word. This conclusion follows from the obligation to avoid harm (here, to keep promises) and to make compensation when injury is done (here, breaking the promise). Notice that this framework does not assume that management decisions can be taken without injury in every case; rather, we must be prepared, when injury does occur, to attend to it. Thus, the company may have no choice but to cut back on orders, but it could still work out a financial compensation with Thompson to make up at least some of the loss.

But Carol is bothered by a deeper level of commitment than explicit promises. Mel reminds her of how much the company has depended on his availability and willingness to be flexible in the past. Carol might also know that Mel has become overly dependent on the company's orders to the great advantage of the company (since Mel's capacity is available to it virtually without competition). She could certainly make the case that special treatment for Thompson Metals is fair because this unique flexibility and relationship is clearly a difference relevant to the plant's productivity.

Commitment and relationships do count for something in the business context. While there is no clear line, Carol quite legitimately ought to ask some questions. How dependent are we on Thompson's flexibility and reliability? How long have we depended on them and what has that meant to their own planning? What will be the impact on Thompson of the cutback in orders? Does Thompson have any alternatives? These questions begin to explore what the commitment between Thompson and the company might mean. The greater the degree to which the plant has been able to use Thompson's commitment to the company as a substitute for having its own in-house capacity, the more the company ought to consider Thompson in a special light. It may not be the same as laying off its own employees or shutting down a division, but neither is it simply a matter of leaving an independent supplier to continue on its independent way.

Notice that the considerations here are ones of degree. Commitment in such cases is seldom absolute or entirely clear. What Carol must do is assess the commitment as a real moral obligation. It is not merely sentiment, as she fears. She needs to make a judgment whether there is sufficient relationship to justify special treatment. And if she decides that Mel is right about the relationship, she must then determine what kind of response is appropriate. The company presumably has limited options, or it would not have directed the cutback to begin with. Carol is challenged to use her imagination to explore with Mel and with Fred Perkins, her immediate boss, what steps might be taken to ease the impact on Thompson Metals. Possibilities might include phasing in the cutback more slowly, shifting some other orders to Thompson, agreeing to tentative new contracts subject to business conditions, and making direct compensatory cash payments. Which option most appropriately fulfills Carol's obligation as purchasing agent for the plant depends on what is possible, what will most assist Thompson, and what will work best for the plant.

Avoiding Harm in Overseas Investment

Evelyn Bates wonders how to sort out her mixed feelings about the proposed South African investment. Is her American company imposing its values if it raises concerns about apartheid in South Africa or one-party regimes in Bulgaria, China, and Mexico? How can her firm be consistently responsible? There is both a role responsibility question here and an underlying query about the meaning of the injunction to do no harm.

The role question is whether Omega can rightly consider domestic political issues in a host country as, in any way, its own problem. The ethical responsibilities framework used here suggests that Omega ought not to do harm, even if other companies might do the business Omega chooses to decline. The impact of Omega's own actions is very much *its* problem. If host country laws mean that Omega will discriminate against employees, Omega "owns" the problem. This is not a self-righteous attitude, but merely the company's effort to fulfill its basic moral obligations. And such an approach does not "impose" Omega's values on the host country or put it in a foreign policy—making role. As an independent firm, Omega can put limits on its own actions. It essentially says, "Here is how we will conduct our business in your country if we are to be there at all." The host country may reply, "Then go elsewhere," and it has that right, but neither the company nor the host government has imposed its values on the other.

So Evelyn can appropriately assess Omega's responsibility in light of the company's values as part of her managerial role. Her questions of ethics arise within Omega's circle of responsibility where its actions might have an impact in the host country. But what does it mean to avoid harm in international investment opportunities?

Some elements are relatively clear: maintaining at least minimum safety standards; providing adequate compensation; dealing honestly and fairly with customers and governments; and adhering to specific policy guidelines (such as those forbidding questionable payments for example). These elements are most clear because they involve direct management actions. If the company is to act ethically, it will be concerned to take such proactive steps to be responsible to its stakeholders. This agenda already raises a number of questions for Evelyn to assess, such as what employment standards will be used in the licensee's plant and whether the office products will be used by agencies that enforce apartheid. But Evelyn's concern to avoid harm extends to Omega's wider impact in its operating presence in South Africa as well. Indeed, this is where Jeff has challenged her.

The company should expect its products and presence to contribute positively to economic development beneficial to host countries. This is part of the basic purpose of the company. To that end, its negotiations with host governments and nationals should seek to fulfill mutually beneficial goals. The more a country's policies appear to frustrate equitable social and political development, the more carefully should the company evaluate whether it can truly avoid harm if it becomes involved with repressive systems.

Assuming a "benign" product such as Omega's office equipment, which can be useful to the efficiency of a variety of business operations, there should be an assumption in favor of doing business in host countries. (This conclusion would differ markedly, depending on the product. Some products, such as strategic military equipment or photographic equipment used to enforce apartheid, would cause direct harm, and the company therefore ought not invest or sell.) Only particularly problematic political or economic circumstances could create conditions where the political-social significance of Omega's involvement constrains its positive economic impact.

But Evelyn must then ask, "Is the situation in South Africa the kind that requires an exception?" What is troublesome is a society that fails to work toward providing basic material needs to its population and/or one whose political system represses the possibility for the development of culturally appropriate, indigenous forms of political expression by its citizens.[6] Such a definition of harm provides a starting point for Evelyn to assess her particular investment opportunity.

In doing so, she will need to ask a number of specific questions, such as:

- What are the dominant characteristics of the host country? On the whole, are there trade-offs between material needs and political rights? Are there particularly troubling repressive patterns?
- What is the historical context and direction? Are conditions getting better or worse? Are there signs of new directions, or do old patterns persist?
- What is the "policy" context? What do policies of the United States government, other nations, and the United Nations suggest about strategies and prospects for change? Are there nongovernmental initiatives that

affect the company's impact (for example, the Sullivan Principles for fair employment practices in South Africa)?

We cannot here spell out the assessment, but we can imagine the concerns Evelyn must consider. She may well conclude that South Africa has an unusually repressive system, that things are getting worse instead of better, and that the general political and policy context means that any new investments will be a symbolic victory for the white regime. On these grounds, Evelyn might turn down the investment opportunity because the business gains to be made are constrained by the obligation to avoid harm.

But Evelyn could also conclude that despite the repressive system, this investment provides jobs to unemployed people in the midst of an uncertain situation. Historical trends, she might have concluded in the early 1980s, are mixed, and positive economic benefits may be helpful, while the international policy context could seem to her ineffective and inconsistent. Following such reasoning, Evelyn might in good faith conclude that the deal is morally acceptable.

In either case, Evelyn might see that Jeff is right about the situations in Bulgaria, China, and Mexico being different. Following the criteria suggested here, she could if necessary assess each of those countries and conclude that different moral constraints and opportunities exist in each one. In all these considerations, Evelyn would be reflecting more carefully on the meaning of the injunction to do no harm in order to make a responsible decision. Reasonable people of goodwill can disagree, as we shall see more fully in the next chapter, but managers will be more responsible as they reflect on the issue with a framework such as this one.

CHAPTER FIVE

What Do Others Think?
Facts, Principles, and Perspectives

Remember Sharon Metzger? She is troubled by the suggestions from her more experienced colleague that corporate
philanthropy is not what it seems to be. She sees a
responsible and sensitive corporate policy, but Gene sees
top managers indulging in their pet projects. She strives to
meet the laudable fund-raising goals of the company's
United Way drive, while Gene fears that individuals will be
subtly coerced to give by watchful supervisors. Who is
right?

If Sharon is using our framework, she will want to know
what others like Gene think. Nevertheless, when these
opinions challenge her own, she is apt to find it unsettling.
Her experience is not atypical. We often disagree about
ethical matters. Sometimes that disagreement is illuminating. Listening to other points of view can shed new light on
our own judgments. On occasion, however, as Sharon
experiences, the disagreement is puzzling and can even lead
to a kind of paralysis. But if we can understand the sources
and reasons for the disagreement, we can often move
beyond the disagreement to judgment and action.

Perhaps Gene and Sharon simply disagree about the
facts. Sharon recites the policy against supervisory pressure
on employees, while Gene insists that it happens. In her

public affairs role, Sharon should investigate Gene's allegations to be sure the policy is, in fact, operating effectively. Sometimes managers can resolve their differences by getting more information in this way. Sharon may learn that Gene is right or may prove him wrong. More often, the "facts" are not clear. What Sharon might consider legitimate exhortation—for example, the CEO, divisional vice-presidents, and department heads making encouraging speeches and urging hundred-percent giving—Gene may view as improper coercion. Their assessment of the facts is influenced by other considerations, and all the information in the world may not change their points of view.

Sharon is naturally more likely to give the benefit of the doubt to management's efforts to make a good showing in the fund drive. Her job is directly associated with the effort, and she spends most of her time working with people who are "on board" with the effort. Gene, on the other hand, operates in the midst of the organization and sees things from the "receiving" end. He may have directly experienced some pressure or know others who have, or who allege such pressure, and he is more likely to identify with this perspective. The facts alone will not illuminate the disagreement if these different vantage points are not recognized and acknowledged. If such differences are recognized, imaginative managers can take advantage of the opportunity to learn from one another. Sharon, for instance, can check her judgment by listening carefully to Gene and trying to see the situation from his point of view.

Or perhaps Gene sees a greater need for more precise rules and greater attention to systematic compliance, while Sharon thinks that general policy guidance together with the good judgment of managers suffices. It may also happen that Gene sees the facts differently from Sharon because of deeper differences in basic orientation to human and corporate affairs. Gene is said to be something of a cynic in the organization, and his view of the facts may well be colored by a general skepticism about the motives of others or the inevitable threat to individuality of organizational power. Sharon, on the other hand, seems more optimistic and open to the opportunities for good that can come from organizational action. Disagreements at this level are more difficult to resolve because they stem from deeply held values and beliefs. Nevertheless, it is always useful to test out the sources of disagreement to see what might be learned from one another.

Why Do We Disagree? Perspectives on Differences

Any decision is shaped by the relationship of several elements, including the facts, ethical principles and the ways they are understood, and personal perspectives based both on roles and on deeper values and world views.[1] Decisions often look as though we simply assess the situation and apply certain ethical principles to reach a judgment. Of course, we do this, but we also know that the way we interpret the "facts" and how we understand ethical principles are influenced by our roles and loyalties and by our most fundamental beliefs.

For instance, ask the marketing managers and the purchasing managers in any large company about appropriate policies limiting the use of meals and gifts in customer-supplier relations. Almost inevitably, the marketing people will advocate a liberal approach, while the purchasing agents will argue for tighter limits. Both deal with the same set of "facts" in the industry, and both may agree that avoiding conflicts of interest is the key ethical principle. But because of their different organizational roles, marketers look to ways to make the customer-supplier relationship run smoothly whereas purchasers look to ways to protect themselves from undue influence by vendors.

Or consider a discussion between human rights advocates and corporate executives about appropriate company policies regarding investment in South Africa. To be sure, the facts are complicated, and one must be well informed. Yet, although many businesspersons and rights advocates have traveled to South Africa on "fact-finding" missions, they often continue to disagree about investment policy. The continuing differences in viewpoint stem, more likely, from their fundamental perspectives, not from the "facts." Businesspersons and human rights advocates move in different circles in their daily rounds, and their perspectives are certainly shaped by these distinct peer relationships. Furthermore, individuals from either arena may differ on interpreting the facts in South Africa as a result of deep differences in basic values and world view. One person may see the overriding issue as fighting communism, while another sees it as bringing self-determination to South African blacks. For both, these perspectives are shaped by deeply rooted values about justice, security, and the very nature of human society.

Our decisions are shaped by all three of these factors—facts, principles, and perspectives—and each factor influences and is influenced by the others as we form our judgments about particular decisions. Attending to all these categories can help managers to identify sources of disagreement and opportunities for common ground as they wrestle with different opinions in making decisions.

We have already seen how the disagreement between

Sharon and Gene can be better understood through these categories. She is genuinely puzzled about what is, in fact, going on and about what standards are legitimate in judging the contributions effort. If she recognizes her own role biases and optimistic outlook, she can try to learn from Gene's different perspective without necessarily giving in to his conclusions. She takes seriously his criticisms of the fund drive and of the motives and nature of senior management philanthropy.

If she then asks about stakeholders, Sharon faces clearly the competing claims that characterize this example. As the public affairs person charged with day-to-day responsibility for the United Way drive and for many corporate grants to charitable institutions and projects, she has several stakeholders to bear in mind. Senior management wants the drive to succeed and to make a variety of grants. These are legitimate corporate efforts to do some good deeds in the community. In this sense, her work involves those activities of the company that reach beyond its circle of direct responsibility. But other stakeholders within the company's circle have other claims. Employees do not want their job performance to be clouded by pressure and negative judgments based on what is, after all, personal giving, and shareholders expect corporate philanthropy to be conducted on behalf of the corporation's relationship to the wider community, if it is to be done at all. And in the community circle outside the company, there are countless institutions and groups who make claims on the company's resources through grant applications. They expect the company to judge their proposals on their merits in light of the company's stated criteria. Sharon's task is to develop programs and make recommendations to the Corporate

Public Affairs Committee (CPAC) that balance all these claims.

On this task and list of stakeholders, Gene and Sharon would presumably agree. Gene's criticism comes in sorting out that balance. Sharon can begin to sort out the balance using the questions about role responsibility and ethical principles in the previous chapter. Most of the activities for which she is responsible represent "good deeds," and her task is to ensure that these are done without violating basic obligations. Therefore, if the United Way drive does, in fact, coerce employees unfairly, she is obliged to limit the fund-raising techniques even if that means a less successful fund drive. This is the meaning of the increasing stringency of obligation as one moves from good deeds to moral obligations. She must, therefore, take Gene's allegations very seriously and assure herself that no such pressure occurs.

The issue turns on what constitutes fair treatment of employees and what limits there should be on corporate encouragement of employees' charitable contributions. I have already suggested how Gene and Sharon might disagree in interpreting these ethical principles because of role biases and basic value orientations. Sharon will have taken seriously the role bias issue if she has begun this reflection we are now exploring. At the deeper level of basic orientations to the world, Sharon and Gene are not likely to change dramatically. If, in shorthand, she is an "optimist" and he a "cynic," they will always have some difference in viewpoint as they approach issues like these.

Disagreements at this basic level are the most difficult to resolve. As the virtually irreconcilable public debate about abortion policy illustrates, there are times when our basic world view so shapes our interpretation of facts and principles that we cannot find common ground. Fortunately, the impact of these deeper perspectives need not prevent finding common ground in most daily interactions and in management decisions. Sharon and Gene, for instance, can probably find an agreeable approach to key decisions and policies even though each approaches the issues differently. But understanding where the other person is coming from can be a great help. Sharon will learn to respond to Gene differently over time as she sees his comments in light of his general outlook.

It is also possible, as Sharon assesses the meaning of fairness and protection of employee privacy, that she and Gene will continue to differ in how the ethical principles are applied. As I suggested earlier, Gene may take a highly structured and logical approach to thinking about morality, while Sharon may be more intuitive. Gene might rely on specific rules, while Sharon may operate more from general principles that serve as rough guides to complex decisions. Given such differences, it is possible that Gene will expect more careful limitations on management efforts on behalf of the fund drive, while Sharon may believe that the general principles suffice to guide and control supervisors.

These comments serve to illustrate how differences in interpreting ethical principles may contribute to disagreements in resolving cases. In fact, Gene and Sharon can probably agree that there are limits to corporate pressure and that Sharon needs to spell these out more carefully to her supervisor and to work with the CPAC on recognizing the problems Gene raises and addressing them with care. And if Gene continues his cynical doubts, he and Sharon may accept that their disagreements are deeply rooted in different perspectives on the relationship of individuals to organizations; they may simply agree to disagree.

Sharon's discussion with Gene about corporate philanthropy illustrates the value of identifying and understanding disagreements in moral questions. It also suggests that recognizing the sources of disagreement can open up opportunities for sharing ideas and gaining new insights. Considering what others think is a key part of ethical decision making in corporate life.

CHAPTER SIX

Am I Being True to Myself?
Integrity and Personal Identity

Should our company lose a major sale because of moral qualms about dealing with Iran during the hostage crisis? The marketing manager and I concluded that the sale was acceptable. The product would be used to supply power to irrigation pumps for domestic agricultural needs. We considered the relevant stakeholders, the company's role responsibility, and the principles involved, and we concluded that the sale was morally permissible because the products were strictly for commercial use of benefit to the general public in Iran. In other words, we did the analysis I have suggested in the preceding chapters. But the senior vice-president in charge of international markets vetoed the plan, saying, "We will not have our company's products shipped to Iran while they hold American hostages. We're not that kind of company." The senior manager recognized an element of the analysis that we had overlooked: How would this action fit into our identity and long-term story?

There is a danger, of course, that such considerations become nothing more than sentiment and personal bias. Perhaps the senior manager was simply being naive and overly sensitive. Certainly, there was nothing wrong in making the sale if the analysis was done responsibly. In this case, either decision was probably morally appropriate. But testing ethical decisions against personal and corporate values and identity is a critical step, and it must always be integrated with the careful reflection outlined in the first five questions of this framework. Responsible ethical decisions result from combining thoughtful analysis with a basic sense of personal and corporate integrity.

We see examples of this dimension with some of our six managers. Wendell Johnson is explicit about this step in his own analysis: "I have met all the requirements of my ethics." Carol Williams almost seems to know that commitment counts for something as she reflects on her conversation with Mel Thompson. She needs the careful analysis to guard against mere sentiment, but she senses she would not be true to herself and the relationship without taking some action to assist Mel. So, too, do Evelyn Bates and Steve Simpson combine their analysis of competing claims with reliance on their own basic values and perceptions of what kinds of actions are consistent with personal and company values. Says Steve, "It was always with doubt: Are we doing the right thing?" Even Charles Warren, who seems to rationalize his way out of the dilemma he clearly feels, does so because he seems desperately to want to find a way to be true to himself.

Would I Tell the Children? Integrity Is the "Bottom Line"

A final step in making ethical decisions, then, is to step back from the cognitive analysis and ask how the proposed action fits into my identity. What kind of person or firm would do this sort of thing? How would I feel if I read about about the decision in the morning paper? Could I comfortably explain the action to my spouse? to my children? These questions are not merely defenses against embarrassment. Rather they are devices to challenge our own self-deception. When we ask such questions honestly, we get underneath the rationalizations that may be leading us astray and remember who we really are. Sometimes the answer confirms helpfully what we have concluded from the earlier questions in the framework. At other times, such as my experience with the Iranian deal, the result is a new perspective on the choices.

Actions, say Oliver Williams and John Houck, "do not really flow from *principles*; rather they flow from *stories*."[1] Ethical principles are integrally related to patterns of life and commitment that take expression in what we normally call character. If principles such as honesty, commitment, and fairness are important guides for moral responsibility, then virtues such as integrity, truthfulness, loyalty, and justice are essential character traits to sustain a moral life. We can say of a particular action, "That was a just act," if the persons involved were treated fairly. But we say of a respected judge or manager, "She is a just person," because of her steady and predictable tendency to treat people fairly in a variety of settings.

Virtues, rather than principles, are the distinctive focus here. Managers cannot act simply out of cognitive assessment of principles as though questions of ethics were merely technical questions. Not only must they reflect carefully; they must also attend to their own deeper values and patterns of acting that shape and sustain their approach to particular questions. We do not so much reason about isolated issues as we live and grow into patterns of integrity and action. The analytic tools introduced in earlier chapters can be taught and "practiced." Character, on the other hand, is built over years of experience and influence from many sources.

Character Makes a Difference: Personal Identity and Ethical Responsibility

William Diehl, a former Bethlehem Steel executive, re-counts his experience of uprooting his family on several occasions to move to new positions within his company. He wondered whether the company, in effect, owned him.

> I began to question myself as to whether I would go anywhere I was asked to go. Would I always say yes? Would the family always have to make the sacrifice in favor of the company?[2]

Finally, he chose to say no to a promotion and move despite the risk that he would be passed over on other occasions.

> I drove home that day with a kind of freedom that I have seldom experienced. I had said no . . . when the stakes were very high. I knew that the company did not own me, nor would it ever. I was free![3]

What made Diehl free to take this decision? Was it a careful weighing of the risks and options? Or was it a keen sense of his own identity and fundamental values? He was able to reach a difficult decision, and to appreciate fully its liberating power only afterward, because of his basic character and identity. A course in ethics would not have helped him very much in struggling with the decision. A lifetime of integrity, of risking commitment, enabled him to say "No!"

Our basic perspectives and self-understanding are shaped by fundamental values and beliefs. For some, the story and experience of religious faith illuminate events in life and enable them to understand their own stories and those of the world around them in a meaningful way. Patterns of spiritual piety and ritual, symbols, and examples and images from religious traditions serve to shape their self-understanding. For others, it is the values fostered and nurtured in family and community that ground their view of the world. These experiences affect how they deal with tragedy and death in close personal circles, what they expect of life in community and institutions, where they gain satisfaction from personal endeavor, and how they grasp hope and possibility in their own lives and in the history of the wider society. Who we are and how we see the world are shaped fundamentally by our most deeply held values.

Our character is strengthened through time as we weave together a series and variety of events, roles, relationships, and commitments. Stories from our family's history, significant events that move or challenge us, and admired teachers, colleagues, and community leaders all help to shape our own attitudes, values, and goals. And this process of character development never occurs only in isolated, private experience. Rather, our identity is shaped through relationships and community involvement as our own story takes its place in the context of the wider story of family and community.

This is why Charles is troubled that his story on the job may conflict with his image of himself. He knows he cannot split his identity between work and home or community. Moreover, his integrity is nurtured and sustained within community. Like Charles, we all need community not only to sustain our own personal character, but also to challenge and support one another.

Personal Character

To return to the beggar on the street corner, some might pass by because they have a well-cultivated suspicion of strangers that disposes them to avoid beggars almost automatically. Others may respond with a gift absentmindedly because of ingrained habits of response to charitable needs. Still others might make a donation or offer to assist the person to a service center because of a steady and clear intention to help others whenever possible. In each case, the response is shaped in large measure by well-established habits of mind and heart. If we knew the individuals, we could probably say with some truth that their actions suited the sorts of persons we knew them to be.

Patterns of living that give expression to deeply held values require dispositions and intentions that lead us to act dependably in light of these values. Dispositions are simply those steady habits of heart and mind, cultivated over a long time, that incline us to act in certain ways. They are often less decisions to act than unself-conscious habitual responses. Intentions are similar, but they refer to more self-conscious aims that we seek to accomplish through particular acts.

Traditionally, these dispositions and intentions have been described as virtues. The word itself derives from a Greek word meaning *excellence* and could refer to any quality that is commendable for a certain purpose, such as speed in an athlete. In the moral context, excellence derives from those habits of mind and heart that dispose one always to act with integrity and high ethical standards. Descriptions of essential virtues display a wide variety. Greek philosophy deemed the so-called cardinal virtues to be temperance, prudence, courage, and justice. Thomas Aquinas suggested that these were, in turn, qualified by the virtues of faith, hope, and charity. But the list of virtues relevant to the moral life is much broader. Typical examples include perseverance, compassion, integrity, candor, fidelity, public-spiritedness, and humility.

Each virtue has its own distinctive quality, and different persons are likely to display more fully some virtues rather than others. We may say of one person that she is a just woman, meaning that her personality and habits of heart and mind lead her to be meticulously fair in dealings with other persons. But the same person may not exhibit the virtues of prudence and temperance with the same distinction. Another may be especially faithful and loyal to friends; he is that kind of person. In each case, the virtue represents a settled disposition more or less "built into" the person's character that disposes him or her both to be a certain kind of person and to act in ways consistent with that identity.

Integrity is perhaps the first among equals among the virtues, for it refers to a kind of wholeness of character itself. The person with integrity acts sincerely and consistently in light of his or her overall values and commitments. "While referring to the self in its wholeness, integrity also points beyond the self toward the person, the ideal, the transcendent which gives shape to the person's life."4 Integrity, then, points to the narrative of one's life in the context of the community.

With integrity and the virtue of courage comes the risk taking that we see in Diehl's career decision. Were we to assume that only "successful" actions were worth trying, we would miss many opportunities for responsible action. We learn that even when we act with integrity, good intentions, and thoughtful reflection, we may fail. But learning that we can survive the failures can give courage to troubled managers who, like Diehl, risk career growth and perhaps even loss of a job to stand up for an important principle.

Well short of such dramatic examples, personal character plays an important, constructive role in management ethics. We noted earlier that the world of the manager is characterized by a rapid flow of often complex and ambiguous problems requiring resolution. It is often difficult to know when to slow down the process to examine something more carefully, and it is easy to make mistakes, with both economic and ethical consequences, as a result. Managers who have cultivated dispositions to act fairly and honestly with integrity are more likely to act ethically in such circumstances than those who have ignored these important character traits. They are also more likely to accept the risk of acting, despite possibilities for failing. Even so prosaic a classical virtue as prudence makes a similar contribution, for prudence in its fullest sense orients us to discerning the world as it is. This means remembering the past and its lessons, discerning the relevant realities in the present, and readying ourselves for the unexpected in the future.[5] All of this is part of the anticipatory management style so crucial to ethical management.

The more often we exhibit the virtues, the more likely we are to act ethically almost without thinking. And when we are grappling with a complex question of ethics, these same character traits become part of our overall process of reflective practice. What kind of person would do this sort of thing? Does this action fit my story and my company's story?

Easier Said Than Done

Why is it so difficult to sustain consistent personal identity and character? There are forces in our experience that work against us. Most important is a radically individualist undercurrent in our culture that threatens to undermine social commitments. This conception of atomistic individuals, which I mentioned briefly earlier, has roots in American political and economic theory, and it is pervasive in contemporary society.[6] It is the dark side of our profoundly important respect for individual liberty.

Relevant here is the tendency, according to Robert Bellah and his associates in *Habits of the Heart,* for individuals to identify their interests in terms of self-expression and tactics to achieve personal or institutional goals. This leads in turn to an erosion of genuine community, which "attempts to be an inclusive whole, celebrating the interdependence of public and private life," and the rise of "lifestyle enclaves," that is, gatherings of persons for essentially private pursuits with others who share similar life-styles.[7] Bellah acknowledges that most groups probably constitute some combination of these two characterizations, but the strength of radically autonomous individualism constantly threatens the community dimension. And yet this is the dimension so crucial to character development, for traditions and stories are carried by communities of memory and hope.

> The communities of memory that tie us to the past also turn us toward the future as communities of hope. They carry a context of meaning that can allow us to connect our aspirations for ourselves and those closest to us with the aspirations of a larger whole and see our own efforts as being, in part, contributions to a common good.[8]

This is why emphasis on integrity within the community is so vital. Community is an antidote or counterforce in a culture dominated more by radical individualism and life-style enclaves than by genuine communities of memory and hope. Only in groups with integrity and deeply rooted traditions of meaning can individual values be shaped and strengthened.

A number of factors in our social environment work against maintaining integrity and developing strong character. William Diehl suggests that such facets of our lives as competition; excessive loyalty to jobs and institutions; and concerns for security, power, and status are cultural forces that often hold us captive without our recognizing their impact.[9] Responsible managers will want to take these forces seriously.

Diehl's story of his refusal to make another move for the company illustrates the point. Demands for commitment of time and energy, for loyalty, and for conformity stemming from the employer or one's own career interests can become overpowering forces that enslave people. Diehl's decision to say no shows what it means to triumph over such powerful social forces. But not everyone finds it possible to say no in the way William Diehl chose, as Charles Warren probably knows better than most. In seeking to strengthen moral responsibility, we cannot lose sight of the forces that constrain individuals, often without their awareness.

In addition to understanding the cultural phenomenon of individualism and the other forces that work against developing integrity, we need to develop a deeper insight into human nature to help us understand the possibilities and limits of character development. Some thinkers, notably the moral psychologist Lawrence Kohlberg, argue that moral development is a process parallel to cognitive development. Individuals move through stages as their powers for rationality mature.[10] While this notion of stages of moral development can be helpful and illuminating, it carries with it undue confidence in the power of reason to recognize and pursue the good. Good intentions and rational moral development alone do not suffice to nurture and sustain moral character.

We all have a human tendency to overestimate our capacity to achieve the good and to underestimate our capacity for harm. Our distinctive fallibility does not stem from perversity or intentionally unethical behavior. These are too obviously a problem, so we recognize them and condemn them. Rather, we are fallible and prone to make mistakes because of the unintended consequences of our well-intentioned actions.[11] We can see this tendency in the innovative product that turns out to have unforeseen safety hazards or the personnel decision that solves one problem only to create new ones. Although we can nurture our moral development as Kohlberg suggests, despite our best efforts, we can no more escape this human limitation in business than in other arenas of life.

So, there are forces that work against the nurture of personal identity and moral character, most notably the individualism so predominant in our culture but also other cultural pressures as well as the characteristic human tendency to fall short of our aspirations. But none of these realities need be decisive. Indeed, they remind us how crucial it is to develop communities of memory and hope, communities of conscience, that strengthen character and support those who are struggling with difficult problems.

How, then, is responsible identity nurtured and sustained in ways that shape the values of corporate managers and support them as they struggle with questions of ethics? For some, there may be no obvious, vigorous, and vital community of conscience in which to participate. They are most at risk of losing perspective. Without the probing challenges and nurturing support from some community or group, their sensitivity to ethical issues and even their fundamental character will erode.

Opportunities for such sustaining community experiences abound if managers recognize their value. Some find help in peer groups that share problems and perspectives together, much the way medical professionals learn from one another by considering cases. Others are involved in growth and support groups that can include consideration of ethical issues. A tightly knit extended family is the community of conscience for some. Still others seek such support in spiritual retreats and religious congregations or gatherings.

Integrity is the "bottom line" in ethical decisions. Asking "Am I being true to myself?" helps us to check our reasoning about a specific case in light of who we are as whole persons. And we will most successfully ask, and answer, the question if our personal identity takes shape through vital relationships in some community of memory and hope.

CHAPTER SEVEN

Now What?
Practical Strategies in the Company and in the Community

The six questions framework introduced in the last several chapters will help managers like Wendell Johnson and Carol Williams make the difficult decisions they face with Mac and Thompson Metals. The framework provides practical ways to help managers identify issues and stakeholders, consider what sort of responsibility they have and what ethical principles mean in concrete situations, work through differences with others, and make decisions with personal integrity. But Wendell and Carol and all of us make decisions in context, not in isolated textbook cases. Having mastered the framework for approaching particular problems, how, as a responsible manager, do you deal with the context of your work? How do you find contexts within the community for supporting your commitment to ethics?

Ethos and Ethics: Corporate Culture and Management Ethics

Suppose Wendell has a pure heart, the best of intentions, and an adept ability to use the six questions framework in resolving questions like his problem with Mac's performance. How could his company help him? How might he learn from his experience to recommend ways the company could be more helpful? My own experience with Cummins Engine Company, as well as observations of many other corporations, suggests how several elements can contribute to sustaining ethical management. Indeed, careful attention to all five of the following elements is essential to creating a context for managers like Wendell to make responsible decisions.

1. Clear corporate ethos that encourages responsible behavior
2. Top management commitment to nurture that ethos
3. Specific policy guidance on difficult issues
4. Staff support to assist line managers on an internal consulting basis
5. Development of managerial awareness and competence through ethics training

These elements are interdependent and, in the contemporary context, resemble a house of cards.[1] No one element alone can create or sustain ethical management, and weakness in even one quality can undermine the whole effort in much the way a house of cards is vulnerable without each of its supporting members.

I use the house of cards metaphor advisedly, not to suggest that business ethics is in any sense a sham, but rather to emphasize the precarious nature of ethical management in the manager's world. Ethics is not yet a regular part of managerial training, nor is a sophisticated and thorough approach to ethics a standard dimension of management practice. Given the pressures of managerial life, therefore, questions of ethics can easily be pushed off the agenda.

Organizational Elements

1. Corporate Ethos.   What kind of company do you work for? Is it the sort of place where you can raise ethical issues and find encouragement? Or would using the ideas in this book be alien in your setting? *Corporate culture* is a familiar term in contemporary management discussions, and like most such notions, the concept highlights an important truth despite the excessive claims typically made for the latest theory. The truth here is that particular organizations do, indeed, have distinctive cultures. Is this the sort of company where Wendell can speak freely to colleagues and to his boss about his ethical concerns? Or, if he does raise the question, do colleagues fidget and stare at the ceiling until the discussion returns to "bottom line" matters?

Consider Cummins as an example. It was founded in the early 1900s by an entrepreneurial chauffeur to the local banking family in the small southern Indiana town of Columbus. Clessie Cummins's venture into diesel engines, financed by the Irwin family, operated at a loss for many years. Early letters and documents make clear that one of the interests of the founders was to provide jobs for local young people. As the company grew under the leadership of J. Irwin Miller, its chairman for more than thirty years, this initial sense of social responsibility was strengthened at every step. The company developed a clear ethos in which ethical responsibility was explicitly affirmed and expected. It was also an ethos that emphasized innovation, product quality, and customer service. That history has continued to shape the company's identity and guide its decisions. Indeed, many managers explain that they decided to join Cummins precisely because of its socially responsible and innovative ethos.

Management consultant and professor James O'Toole sees corporate culture at work in what he calls "vanguard companies," such as Atlantic Richfield, Control Data, Dayton-Hudson, Deere, Honeywell, Levi Strauss, Motorola, and Weyerhaeuser.[2] O'Toole identifies these examples in the first instance by simply asking people where they would choose to work if they could pick any one large American company. "Uneasy about this list?" he asks. "Think about it. What would you look for in a potential employer?" He suggests factors such as corporate procedures and policies consistent with one's own values, good benefits, successful products, opportunity for interesting and challenging work, flexible working conditions, high morale, and strong ethical commitments. Corporate culture is identifiable even without elaborate social-scientific approaches. It is the tangible "feel" of a place and how it operates. It is evident in how jobs are designed, how people are treated in communications and decision-making processes, how customers and suppliers are dealt with, and how people in the company think about themselves and their relationships to one another, to business associates, and to the community.

Each company has its own history, its own distinctive story, that has helped to shape its contemporary identity and ethos. This identity contributes to shaping individual role behavior into organizational action rather than simply personal decisions. Where that ethos encourages ethical management, it can be lifted up, celebrated, and reinforced. In such a culture, Evelyn and Wendell and Sharon and Carol can pursue their questions of ethics without embarrassment or resistance. Steve Simpson's actions in the Sun Ship closing appear to reflect such a positive culture as he sought to carry out the painful task with a sense of responsibility.

Where the culture is indifferent or even perhaps hostile to ethics, responsible managers would have greater difficulty. It may simply be unheard of to raise such questions of ethics in management discussions. Even to admit to these concerns might mark you as at best eccentric and at worst insufficiently devoted to corporate success. Charles Warren appears to operate in such a culture, at least to the extent that he is pressured to take unethical actions because he feels this is "playing ball" with the ways things are done in his company.

Any efforts to strengthen ethical management must attend to corporate history and culture. Steve Simpson may perceive a positive culture when middle managers and/or people at the bottom might be more ambivalent about the organization's ethos. Given the isolation of top management, corporate culture and ethos are probably best assessed from the bottom up. This is where managers like Wendell not only benefit from working within a positive culture but where they can help to create and sustain such a culture in their own divisions and departments and try to communicate problem areas to higher management levels. If the setting is less than fully supportive, there may still be resources in the company's history or in the industry's history and practice that they could appeal to in making arguments for particular policies and approaches.

2. Top Management Commitment. The CEO of Evelyn's company once turned down an investment in South Africa, saying, "Nobody said we have to be the biggest company in the world." That story is significant to Evelyn and to Jeff because it means top management will take their concerns seriously. Less positively, the CEO's actions are under special scrutiny in tough cases, and even the perception that ethics have been compromised will undermine commitment to ethics lower in the organization. In more recent discussions, for instance, Evelyn's CEO was open to some South African business, a stance that led some managers to argue that ethical considerations were out and profitability was the only consideration.

The importance of senior management's commitment to ethics is virtually a platitude, but no less important for that. Conscientious chief executive officers cannot, alone, impose ethical management, but their initiative and support are essential. The CEO needs to be articulate, visible, and firm in explaining corporate philosophy and policies, reinforcing commitment to those policies regularly and upholding the philosophy and policy in tough cases. Examples of instances in which the CEO has supported ethics, even at a financial loss, become part of the lore of the organization and give support to middle-level managers as they, in turn, seek to uphold ethical practices.

Cummins Engine Company is an excellent example of the importance of senior management's commitment. J. Irwin Miller became CEO in the early 1930s, when the company was still a small operation. At the helm during the company's rapid growth in the 1950s and 1960s, Miller was clear and vigorous in his insistence that high ethical standards be maintained in business dealings. His personality and leadership were critical contributions to the developing ethos of the organization, and he understood the importance of top management in this process. As he once noted, " 'All of the corporate standards of ethics don't mean anything unless the persons in the corporation perceive the top people to abide by them when the going is really tough.' "[3]

This affirmation of top management's commitment ought not to be focused exclusively on the CEO. In most major corporations, senior managers for various functional areas (for example, the persons with overall responsibility for marketing, manufacturing, and research) play leadership roles in their divisions akin to the role of the CEO in the whole corporation. Their role in supporting ethical management is nearly as critical as that of the CEO. As a group, senior management plays a crucial role in modeling ethical behavior as it decides central policy issues and strategic plans. Likewise, divisional and department heads have a similar impact on the subculture of their own areas. In this sense, Evelyn's decision on South Africa and Wendell's resolution of his problems with Mac will send signals to each one's own group about the meaning of ethical commitment. Any manager who supervises even one person has opportunity for setting a consistent tone for ethical behavior.

A word about so-called whistleblowing policies provides an appropriate transition here from top management's commitment to ethical management to the subject of policy guidance. As senior managers seek to reinforce ethical management, perhaps nothing sends so powerful a message as a serious effort to hear and act on concerns raised by responsible lower-level managers. The senior person who does not want to hear about questions of ethics quickly convinces subordinates that ethical behavior is acceptable only if it does not reduce immediate profits or cause headaches for higher levels. Furthermore, as Barabara Toffler points out, the "I don't want to know about that" reaction of a senior manager is often nothing more than a way to sidestep responsibility.

> It just may be that not wanting to know is the surest sign that attention ought to be paid. While we can agree that no one can know everything, the choice to want to know more

than "just the bottom line" is essential to creating an ethically capable organization.[4]

The executive who reinforces managers who report questionable practices or who raises ethical concerns as part of the business analysis can convince subordinates to risk raising questions in ambiguous situations. Clear policy commitments that encourage such question raising and seek to protect subordinates when they do raise questions are important here. One company states it this way:

> No employee will suffer a career disadvantage for failing to carry out an instruction which he or she believes to be morally inappropriate or for raising questions about a corporate practice which he or she believes is morally dubious.[5]

Charles Warren might be helped by such a policy and by having an appropriate person to contact the next time he is pressured to alter production reports. But senior managers need to recognize that protection is not always possible, that persons may risk subtle reprisals if they raise certain issues. We might say from the safe distance of an armchair that Charles ought to "blow the whistle" on his supervisor. But even if Charles's company has adopted a policy encouraging such action, he may well wonder whether his supervisor or other powerful managers in his division will find ways to hold such action against him later in his career. Special vigilance in encouraging the raising of ethical issues and monitoring the protection of those who risk criticizing the ways things are done is essential, the more so given the isolation of people at the top.

3. Policy Guidance.   Many companies adopt codes of ethics, and there is often a debate about whether codes will make corporations ethical. Posed in that way, the question is not very helpful. Of course, a code will not guarantee ethical management, for policies do not automatically yield compliance. Indeed, a code without any efforts at compliance would do more harm than good. But codes and policy guidance are important elements in the whole process of ethical management. As we have seen, managers discover questions of ethics in the midst of their responsibilities, and policy guidance can help to answer some of them.

General ethical principles embodied in a code or policy statement serve to remind employees of the company's commitment unambiguously. This may be a brief and simple statement such as Johnson and Johnson's decades-old credo (which cites in less than a page the company's commitment to customers, employees, communities, and stockholders) or a more elaborate discussion of rationale and key principles. The importance of such statements should be appreciated but not overestimated. Without the other elements described here, a general philosophy statement neither helps people determine what to do nor encourages them effectively to act ethically. But a vigorously supportive CEO who never puts anything down on paper risks not being taken seriously and tying the ethics commitment too much to his or her own personality. Wendell will feel encouraged to consider ethical treatment of Mac if the company has articulated its basic philosophy and communicated it effectively throughout the organization.

Policies ought also to move beyond general philosophy into particular issues where specific policy guidance can be given to managers. Irwin Miller notes, "Dr. [Samuel] Johnson says we need more often to be reminded than informed."[6] Policies can remind managers of certain areas for which the duties and obligations are clear, such as not accepting personal favors in exchange for business or detailed definitions of actions that could be construed as violating antitrust laws. In addition, policy guidance can assist managers who are puzzled about the meaning of particular principles in light of a broad "do good and avoid harm" philosophy statement. Policies also help the busy manager to identify those areas where he or she must slow down the decision process and do so without apology.

Cummins Engine Company has not only a general policy statement but also specific policies on topics selected according to the line managers' perception of their need for guidance. That is, particular questions of ethics encountered in carrying on the business of the company gave rise to policies intended to help individual managers resolve questions in such areas as political participation, questionable payments, meals and gifts, and defense sales. In some cases, the policies give very specific definitions, prohibitions, and procedures (for example, concerning so-called facilitating payments overseas); in other cases a general principle is described and illustrated as the basis for continual judgment calls by managers (for instance, meals and gifts with customers and suppliers).

Obviously, policies cannot cover every managerial decision. If they could, the problem of sustaining ethical management would be simplified immeasurably. The importance of developing some explicit ethics policies is twofold. First, the very act of being explicit and specific beyond the philosophy statement tells managers that the company is serious about its philosophy. And, where policies can be developed, managers have greater guidance in making difficult decisions and some assurance that they will be supported by senior management where a tough decision guided by a policy yields some disappointing financial results. This is a two-way street, for top management officers reduce their own isolation from organizational realities as they try to develop policies that genuinely address the problems of middle managers. Referring to the commitment that must underlie such policies, Irwin Miller notes,

> If in doubt, you should share the responsibility right up to the top of the company. And along with that would go a growing conviction in the company, which takes years to build, that under certain circumstances you're willing to lose the order. You can never stop teaching that. . . . The only thing that really means anything . . . is a long history and experience of examples in which a management acted exactly that way.[7]

If policies are developed in such a context, both middle managers and top management strengthen their confidence in addressing questions of ethics.

In fact, one strategy for initiating greater sensitivity to ethical management, even in a company whose culture has been historically indifferent to ethics, is to canvass managers about areas where they are puzzled about their decisions and would welcome policy guidance. Developing policies in response to this process and working to interpret and implement them can contribute to cultural change and reinforce ethical management.

4. *Staff Support.* If Carol Williams wants some help in thinking about Mel Thompson's request for special consideration in the plant purchasing cutback, whom can she call? At Cummins Engine Company, Harry was able to call the Corporate Responsibility Department. Its purpose is to support ethical management throughout the organization in

three ways. One task is policy development and interpretation. The department provides staff support to management in developing particular policies, takes initiative in making policies known to employees, and assists line managers in interpreting the policies in particular cases. Second, the department serves as a consulting resource to managers at every level on questions of ethics in business decisions. Managers often need an outside perspective to help them think through difficult or puzzling issues. This assistance ranges from a telephone conversation or brief meeting to long-term involvement on a project team assessing a major business decision or policy question. Finally, the department works on management education and development.

While Cummins has created a separate Corporate Responsibility Department, other companies fulfill some or all of these functions through different staff groups. Personnel, public affairs, community relations, and law departments are examples. Some organizations have an ombudsperson to help spot problem areas and offer support to aggrieved or puzzled employees. Wherever the responsibility is lodged, staff support capable of helping managers in these three tasks is an essential component of ethical management. Managers can and will act ethically without any help, but the staff support strengthens their ability to do so.

Charles Warren might not want to risk it, but at least he could go confidentially to some such staff person for advice and, perhaps, even protection in addressing his dilemma. Carol Williams and Wendell Johnson might well find it useful to discuss their questions of ethics with a knowledgeable corporate staff person, one whose role is not to decide for them or to instruct them from higher moral ground, but rather to assist them in considering what commitment and fairness might mean in these cases. It may well be that the staff person has had experience with others in similar situations that might shed light on the immediate problems. They might even think together whether their particular questions give rise to policy issues that the staff person could pursue and develop (for instance, working with their personnel departments to assess the adequacy of current policy and procedures for performance evaluation and termination). Likewise, Sharon Metzger and Evelyn Bates might naturally turn to someone in a staff role to help them sort out their questions of competing claims. Evelyn's work with Jeff Seltzer already illustrates one effort on her part to sound out ideas with a specialized staff person. As general counsel, Steve Simpson already represents, to some extent, one sort of staff resource to management decisions, and that may be one reason he was chosen to manage the Sun Ship closing. The parent company could learn from this experience if Steve or some other staff person seeks to develop new contingency policies and plans for future downturns or plant closings. For all these managers, the key point about staff support is that there actually is someone to call and ask for advice, background research, and information and someone to help in looking at the implications of a given decision.

5. *Education and Development.* Regardless of a company's policies and procedures, ethical management still rests finally on individual judgments throughout the organization. Therefore, recruiting ethically sensitive managers and supporting the development of their ethical judgment is a final critical element. Recruitment decisions are always complicated, but a company can be clear about its values, and interviewers can be alert to the applicant's values in an effort to recruit managers who are committed to the same

basic ethical principles as is the company. One chief executive says that a critical quality of new employees ought to be a "capacity for moral outrage," that is, the willingness to raise questions of ethics rather than bury them. Though difficult to "measure" or identify in the abstract, this characteristic is symbolic of the crucial dimensions of personal character and integrity needed for ethical management.

More manageable, perhaps, is the task of supporting managers once they are part of the company. Educational programs are an essential component in strengthening ethical management. Training enhances awareness and skills in dealing with ethical issues in management, and it exposes managers to staff resources for seeking assistance when they encounter difficult issues in the future. Many companies have developed such programs, in some cases focused on disseminating and interpreting policies and in others taking a broader approach to ethics and corporate values. At Cummins Engine Company, workshops for managers are designed to provide practical conceptual tools for addressing questions of ethics in the corporate context. The seminars also create a network of managers in the company who can be resources to one another and who know about the corporate responsibility staff resource.[8] Off-site programs can also be useful. Douglas Wallace, for example, has designed an integrated curriculum for managers that begins with analytic tools but moves into deeper levels of "ethical sharpening, perspective deepening, and moral courage."[9] These parts of the program use literary and dramatic materials, social-psychological tools, readings in philosophy, and ongoing group meetings to help individuals strengthen their own sense of integrity and identity.

Performance assessment, rewards, and punishments can

also contribute to sustaining and strengthening ethical commitment in management. Explicit incentives and sanctions are sometimes used with great effect when they can be targeted to particular issues. Peter T. Jones recounts his efforts at Montgomery Ward's to ensure compliance with equal pay laws in the early 1970s. Even after strong policy pronouncements, follow-up auditing showed that some ten percent of store managers had ignored the policy. These managers were docked $5,000 to $10,000 from their annual bonuses, and, despite initial reactions that this penalty was unfair, Jones suggests that the sanctions made clear that the company expected its managers to live up to the policy. The next step was to put the bonus money in escrow as an incentive; if the managers brought their pay scales into compliance within the next year, they could earn their bonuses back. Virtually all of them did.[10]

Even without such a precise carrot and stick, companies can encourage ethical commitment by giving attention to a manager's record on questions of ethics in considering promotions and by making clear its displeasure at ethically insensitive actions through reprimands and, in certain cases, even termination. The promotion of a manager who has missed a market target because of ethical considerations signals that the company stands behind its commitments. If the manager is passed over, however, for someone who clearly worries little about questions of ethics, a contrary message will be equally clear. And here, the strategies for supporting ethical management take us back to corporate culture.

We sometimes speak of institutionalizing management ethics, that is, building the process of ethical management into the systems, structures, and culture of an organization. If that effort is successful, management ethics will be sustained without depending unduly on a particular personality in the organization or an unusual time in the company's history. The five elements I have outlined are vehicles for institutionalizing ethics. As such, they contribute to shaping an ethical organization whose managers fulfill their roles with ethical sensitivity. You can use the list to identify strengths and weaknesses in the company or in your own department, and you can seek to strengthen one or another element as opportunities allow.

The company that attends explicitly and in depth to these five elements begins to build ethics into its culture. Each element is crucial and depends, in important ways, on all the other elements. Where top management is committed but fails to provide staff support and ethics training, the effort will fall short of the CEO's dreams. And where a staff department initiates effective training without a clear policy framework and senior-level support, the result may simply be frustrated managers. But the more effectively a company addresses all of these elements, the stronger the foundation of ethical management from top to bottom.

Recognizing Obstacles to Management Ethics

Managers discover questions of ethics in the fabric of their business activities, and they typically accept some responsibility for resolving such questions. The organizational elements I have outlined will help people like Wendell and Carol and Evelyn to address their questions in a supportive context. But a caution is in order before we proceed, for there are obstacles to all of these well-intentioned efforts. Consider how difficult it is to make good ethical judgments in the manager's world.

The complexity and ambiguity of many decisions reflect

reality. A senior executive has to decide whether current and upcoming business conditions warrant calling for a layoff. The ethical implications are profound, since many people may suffer because of her business judgment, and needlessly so if she is wrong. Yet that judgment is a difficult one. The sheer size of many corporate organizations, the complexity of their products and communications systems, the uncertainties of information, and the rapidly changing world around the company all make it difficult for even the most conscientious manager to make good judgments every time. The world is complicated, and we are finite human beings, so we make mistakes.

Our natural limitations are also involved in coping with the rapid flow of management decisions and the necessity for action. In the fast-paced, goal-directed activity of management, it is difficult to focus on broader questions, to discern hidden dimensions of a decision. Even responsible managers simply miss a good deal in the flow of information across their desks. The marketing director for an overseas region, for instance, may be so preoccupied with twenty different orders and negotiations on a given morning that he fails to notice an order with questionable social-political or ethical implications.

The goal is to build ethical sensitivity into management so integrally that these issues emerge naturally in the same way that financial concerns arise now. But, at present, even the best and most responsible managers have to be reminded to raise their sights. Here is yet another reason for policy guidance and staff support. Often it is the different perspective from a staff group or policy process that highlights a dimension the line manager has missed.

In addition, the natural human tendency to make mistakes in the pursuit of well-intentioned goals poses another obstacle. Indeed, managerial responsibility within a large organization poses a particular danger. Excessive loyalty to narrowly conceived organizational goals can lead well-intentioned individuals to take actions toward those goals that most persons would condemn from a broader perspective. A good example of how unfortunate such "loyalty blinders" can be is provided in a *Wall Street Journal* account of General Electric's problems with price fixing, bribery, and fraud some years ago.[11] In each case, executives took actions that were unethical and often illegal, despite firm corporate policies on legal compliance and ethical behavior. Although some of the individuals may well have been intentionally unethical, it is more likely that most simply failed to look beyond the immediate opportunity to serve the corporation's best interests as they saw them. Self-deception—belief that their actions would really help the company, that they were not really wrong, that the company would want them to act this way—led executives to unethical actions even with strong policy guidance.

Awareness of these obstacles should not be read as a counsel of despair. It is, rather, a reminder that humility is one of the virtues that characterize those who seek to strengthen ethical management. Ethical management can be strengthened, both by the organizational elements described in this chapter and by the resources for individuals discussed in the next section. At the same time, we want to remember how far we must travel, in a given company and across industry and commerce, to achieve significant improvements in ethical management, and we want to recognize the obstacles to avoid discouragement or premature self-congratulation.

Sustaining Personal Identity: Communities of Conscience

Meanwhile, what am I to do when confronted with tough questions of ethics on a daily basis? If Wendell cannot easily raise his concerns at work, where can he turn? How does Charles get support to deepen his sense of personal identity and find the moral courage to confront his problems at work? Perhaps the most important practical strategy, in light of the importance of community in sustaining character, is to participate in small groups that enable regular sharing, support, study, and accountability. For some, these communities of conscience may arise within churches, synagogues, and other religious groups; others may find them with family or like-minded friends and peers or in various other support groups.

What responsible managers most need to sustain those qualities of character so vital to ethical management, as well as to assess difficult questions of ethics, is an ongoing experience with a group that shares values and concerns. Such groups are necessarily small enough to allow for full individual involvement, say six to twelve persons, and they are disciplined in the sense that group members are seriously committed to the life and tasks of the group. This discipline includes time commitment, regular attendance, and willingness to do the work required. The work may include study and preparation or simply openness to vulnerability in sharing problems and concerns. And a small, disciplined group that shares basic values and purposes will, through time, become a genuine community; that is, it will increasingly be a setting in which mutual care and support arises naturally, in which identity is shaped and values are reinforced or changed.

Groups will develop their own distinctive patterns of life. In general, the focus will be on responsible living in managerial roles, but there may be a rhythm, for individuals and for the group, in which attention focuses on different facets of the experience. Particular questions of ethics faced by one or more persons may be the agenda at one point, whereas deeper study and consideration of philosophical or spiritual themes encountered in discussion of these problems might be the focus at another point. The group may be counseling and nurturing a colleague at one point and challenging the same person at another time.

William Diehl gives two examples of how important this kind of process can be. In one instance, a group of managers met regularly over lunch to share concerns. When they discussed such topics as how to treat poorly performing employees, the group provided an unusual chance for the managers to share the practical meaning of their values with one another. "No list of rules emerged . . . but we did leave . . . with some new things to think about as each of us faced our supervisory responsibilities."[12]

In another city, Diehl participated in a support group and shared a very difficult personnel problem with which he was struggling. It was a diverse group, occupationally, and the discussion helped him by "asking unexpected questions, probing all the alternatives."[13] He went on to make a difficult decision to demote the manager. Recognizing that not everyone would agree, Diehl expresses satisfaction that the support group process deepened his confidence in making a responsible choice. Moreover, the group continued to express concern about the employee in the ensuing years, and Diehl kept them posted. This illustrates not only the support but also the accountability that such a group can provide.

Further affirmation of this emphasis on small groups comes from a study focusing specifically on "transformative education," that is, educational experiences designed to impact the character, values, and behavior of participants on peace and justice issues.[14] Alice and Robert Evans and William Kennedy review a range of exemplary programs and begin to suggest some criteria for effective educational experiences that have the best chance to impact people profoundly. Among the key factors are commitment of time and energy, communities of support and accountability, vulnerability and risk, integration of study/action/reflection, and experiential immersion in dramatically different environments.[15] While the programs considered focus primarily on issues of peace and justice, I think the criteria support the use of small, disciplined communities for strengthening responsible managers as well.

Commitment of time and energy is more important than we might realize, for corporate managers especially understand the "value" of time. The greater the personal investment, the more meaningful will be the experience.

And this commitment needs to be to a community that will support its members in their learning and struggle as well as hold them accountable to their own values and resolutions. In programs as diverse as Bread for the World, a "parenting for peace and justice project," and a project on plant closings, the study of transformative education found that ongoing communities were essential to enabling individuals to sustain the courage and convictions necessary to carry on. This is as true for corporate managers struggling with questions of ethics as it is for a group of activists carrying out a social change strategy.

One can well imagine the help and encouragement Carol Williams or Wendell Johnson might get from such a group, not only in the midst of the problem, but down the road. To share with a group in confidence their concerns and struggles and to report to them on occasion new developments with Thompson Metals and with Mac is a way of ensuring continuity in their own personal stories. Mel and Mac may or may not disappear from Carol's and Wendell's managerial responsibility, but the experience will remain with them for better or worse. Participation in a small community of conscience where they can share such struggles and shape their character and patterns of managing could strengthen them immensely.

Kennedy and Evans also found that vulnerability and (modest) risk taking were critical factors in genuine learning. "Without one's adrenalin running it is difficult to be turned around, to be able to challenge the traditional and become open to the new."[16] The examples in *Pedagogies for the Non-Poor* focus particularly on the physical and psychic risks involved in such activities as picketing and immersion trips into third-world environments. But if it is vulnerability and risk that help engender learning and growth, then most corporate managers are poised for learning. Not only does their job often entail commercial and economic risk, but more important, they sometimes face great personal risk to career and family as they struggle with questions of ethics. This is particularly evident in Charles Warren's case, but certainly Evelyn Bates wonders whether her action will affect her career advancement, and Sharon Metzger must be concerned about how far to press senior management without overstepping an invisible line. The more a small community can develop sufficient trust among its members, the more likely that individuals will share their deeper concerns and take the risks that can lead to new insight and conviction.

While some of these considerations emphasize experiential and relational factors, the study of transformative education also suggests the need for critical analysis and reflection as part of an integrated process. It is the interaction among experience, study, reflection, and action that leads to genuine learning that can impact one's values and behavior. Immersion in another culture or engagement in a social action alone may move a person deeply, but only when this profound experience is woven together with data, analysis, and reflection will the entire process have a lasting impact. Similarly with small groups for businesspersons, the reality of their experiences in management animate the discussion and ground their participation. But part of being a disciplined community is to take care to assess the issues and to reflect carefully on them. Had Steve Simpson been in such a group as he developed his plans for managing the closing of Sun Ship, for instance, we can imagine that the group could have been helpful in assessing the stakeholders, particularly the community needs, and helping Steve to assure himself about the fairness of his decisions. William Diehl's report of his group experience with a difficult personnel issue shows the same contribution of analysis and reflection.

The Kennedy and Evans study suggests, finally, that significant change occurs in assumptions and perceptions when people encounter the poor directly and when they are immersed in another culture. Most dramatic are third-world immersion trips designed to shake prior assumptions and to open individuals to new ways of understanding justice in the global perspective. From these findings, we can learn two things for groups of managers. One is the value of participation in some such activities, possibly independent from the small, disciplined community of corporate managers. One group cannot accomplish all things, and individuals may find participation in a traveling seminar to the third world or some other immersion experience to be very important in their moral development and behavior. Such experiences would enrich the small group's life over time.

Second, such a small group of corporate managers ought to be challenged by this criterion to find ways to open themselves to new perspectives. This might mean changing the composition of the group to include persons from different vocations and economic strata, or it might suggest that the group find ways to experience their own corporate realities in new ways by, for instance, spending time on the shop floor or in working-class neighborhoods. The point from the *Pedagogies* study relevant here seems to be twofold. There is "shock value" in such new experiences that may in itself open up perspectives. In addition, intentional efforts to expose themselves to the realities of other stakeholders may help to form their judgments in new ways as they grow in understanding.

Small support groups, then, can strengthen the character and moral judgment of corporate managers. The key elements are clear: steady commitment to sharing and supporting one another through time in a small community context informed by shared values. How these elements are realized can vary greatly, depending on particular settings and opportunities. Some may meet regularly with friends and colleagues for breakfast or lunch near their workplaces, while another group might convene around their common work in a particular company or industry. Others may meet in homes with family and friends. Still others may develop such groups in the context of religious congregations. Small groups devoted to social action concerns, perhaps relating directly to economic justice issues, might also provide helpful challenges and new insights to business managers. Conferences, retreats, and other short-term educational programs can also contribute to managerial character development and moral judgment. Such activities are no substitute for ongoing involvement in a small group, but they serve at least two important purposes. For those who have other support networks, specific programs may provide helpful resources for thinking about key issues, such as worker participation or plant closings. Second, such programs offer opportunities to lift up to the community the issues and needs of ethics in management, to encourage others to become involved in communities of conscience, and to engage all program participants in better understanding key issues and challenges.

These suggestions for supporting ethics within organizations and for participating in communities of conscience to sustain personal integrity complete our consideration of resources for responsible management. Managers can work to strengthen the key elements in their organizations that build ethics into the fabric of management, and they can use the six questions framework within that fabric to resolve particular issues. They will be supported in these efforts as they also participate in some kind of group that nurtures, challenges, and holds them accountable to their own standards of ethics.

The suggestions here give you some ideas about next steps in strengthening responsible management. Now it's up to you.

Epilogue
Six Managers Revisited

What would it mean for the six managers whose questions of ethics we have considered throughout this book if they were part of a small community of conscience that sought to support one another? Let us suppose, for the sake of illustration, that they, together with a few others, meet regularly with the sorts of commitments and purposes described in the last chapter. Discussions in the group would range much more widely than the particular issues we have examined, but as the participants share their concerns and struggles, each of the six might well share his or her question in much the way it was described in chapter 1.

If the group had studied the resources in this book, they might well begin to respond by seeking to clarify the nature of the problem. Is it really an issue? As I have suggested earlier, that discussion might well focus on single principle issues with Carol and Wendell and on competing claims with Evelyn, Steve, and Sharon. The group discussion might help to clarify these characterizations or to suggest a different perspective. Someone might suggest that Carol think more about fairness issues to other suppliers, for example. For these five, in any case, the discussion about the nature of the issue will quickly lead into the next steps of identifying stakeholders and considering the nature of their responsibility. These steps are necessary to clarify the issue further.

But when Charles Warren shares his dilemma, the group is likely to spend far more time assessing what kind of problem he faces and, in a sense, jumping over the analytical questions to the concern about being true to oneself. As noted earlier, Charles probably needs to confront his situation with less self-deception, to admit that he is being forced into behavior he knows is unethical. A community of supportive colleagues is one of the few settings in which he is likely to expose this to other persons and even to himself. One of the greatest values of ongoing, small, disciplined communities such as this is precisely that they become not only communities of conscience but also communities of support in which a troubled manager can begin to acknowledge difficult personal dilemmas and experience acceptance and understanding. One can imagine, for example, a series of meetings in which Charles moves from defensiveness to recognition of his rationalization and then slowly to a stronger self-image and specific ideas for changing his situation. As he then moves through subsequent events, perhaps challenging his supervisor or going around him, or even changing jobs, the group would be there both to hold him accountable to his intentions and to support him in the difficult moments.

Meanwhile, Wendell or Carol might have shared their questions of ethics and moved together with the group into assessing who is affected by their actions and what sort of responsibility they might have. I illustrated the conclusions of such discussions in chapter 4, focusing on fairness in Wendell's case and on commitment in Carol's situation. Whatever decisions Carol and Wendell take, their judgment will be better grounded in responsible living because of these discussions. And even though they cannot bring every such decision to the group, the discussion, as well as their participation in similar discussions about other people's problems, will contribute to their habits of heart and mind in carrying out their managerial roles in the complex and rapidly flowing environment of business life.

When Sharon, Evelyn, and Steve share their concerns, the group is connected not only through their mutual commitment but also by community involvements. They are familiar with the contributions program of Sharon's company and may even help other groups to seek funds. They know about the divestment controversy regarding South Africa. And, assuming Steve's case concerns a local company, they are part of the same community. As the group discusses relevant stakeholders in each case, they can be especially helpful to one another since they know some of the stakeholders and may, in fact, be stakeholders themselves. In this way, especially in towns and cities smaller than the largest metropolitan areas, such small communities can genuinely become part of the fabric of the wider community in which local companies and regional offices operate. The managers involved are not only sustaining their own values and judgment; they are also contributing to an environment of responsible business.

In Sharon's case, the group's discussion could generate new ideas for her thinking. Most important for Sharon, however, may be the group's ongoing support if she decides on a strategy to push her supervisor and the senior management committee to consider new approaches to philanthropy. This can be risky business for her. The group cannot remove the risk, but it can help her assess what to do and stand with her through the process.

Evelyn brings to the group her practical management experience with an issue that is frequently debated in the larger community. Most important for her, initially, will be the group's willingness to listen to her own struggle without prejudging. A casual conversation at a social occasion is likely to bring a categorical condemnation of doing business in South Africa. Evelyn is genuinely perplexed and will not be helped by that kind of response. In the small group, she can lay out her conflicting impressions and test them with the group. In chapter 4 I illustrated some of the relevant considerations that might arise. The group may well have others with experience in these matters, and it can call on other resource people in the community to learn more about the issue if need be.

Most important, the discussion of this case will help to shape every member's conscience with respect to global realities. Other managers may have occasions to deal with similar issues, and all the participants are also citizens in the wider community. In these roles, too, they must live out their identity as Americans in an increasingly interdependent global society. In-depth discussions about a case such as Evelyn's contribute to the deeper values and perspectives participants bring to all their roles.

Were Steve Simpson in the hypothetical community involved here, his concerns might well have dominated the group's life for some time, given the magnitude of the decision and its impact on the community of which all the members are a part. Experiences such as Steve's have a great impact on personal character and identity. They become part of one's story for better and worse in the months and years that follow. Ongoing participation in a group would reinforce that impact in ways consistent with a person's values and personal identity.

These are but six small plots in six complex stories of corporate managers. They, like anyone with management responsibility, carry on the next day with new issues, dilemmas, and opportunities. Participation in a community of conscience that addresses such issues is essential to strengthening the ability of managers to act responsibly. This book is not intended to solve the problems of Steve and Evelyn, Carol and Wendell, or Charles and Sharon. It is an invitation to you to grapple with your own practical and concrete questions of ethics.

Notes

Chapter One

1. Each of these descriptions is based upon real persons and real events. Three are based on interviews with the individuals themselves published in Barbara Ley Toffler, *Tough Choices: Managers Talk Ethics* (New York: John Wiley and Sons, 1986), and in David Freudberg, *The Corporate Conscience: Money, Power, and Responsible Business* (New York: American Management Association, 1986). In the Toffler work, Charles Warren and Wendell Johnson are fictitious names for real persons. Freudberg details the actual Sun Ship case, using Steve Simpson's real name. The stories of Carol Williams, Sharon Metzger, and Evelyn Bates are composite stories reflecting numerous examples and issues I have encountered working with managers.
2. This case description is summarized from the interview with Charles Warren in Toffler, *Tough Choices*, pp. 79–92.
3. Toffler, *Tough Choices*, p. 82.
4. Toffler, *Tough Choices*, p. 84.
5. Toffler, *Tough Choices*, p. 84.
6. Based on the interview with Wendell Johnson in Toffler, *Tough Choices*, pp. 98–104.
7. Toffler, *Tough Choices*, pp. 100–101.
8. Toffler, *Tough Choices*, p. 102.
9. Toffler, *Tough Choices*, pp. 103–4.
10. Based upon narration and interviews with Stephen W. Simpson, Clarence Moll, and Marie Riley-Pierce in Freudberg, *Corporate Conscience*, pp. 89–111.
11. Freudberg, *Corporate Conscience*, p. 93.
12. Freudberg, *Corporate Conscience*, pp. 96–97.
13. Freudberg, *Corporate Conscience*, p. 98.
14. Freudberg, *Corporate Conscience*, p. 95.

Chapter Two

1. William E. Diehl, *Christianity and Real Life* (Philadelphia: Fortress Press, 1976), p. 37.
2. Attributed to Warren Bennis, cited in Rosabeth Moss Kanter and Barry A. Stein, *Life in Organizations: Workplaces as People Experience Them* (New York: Basic Books, 1979), p. 315.
3. Kermit Vandivier, "Case Study—The Aircraft Brake Scandal," in *Ethical Issues in Business: A Philosophical Approach*, ed. Thomas Donaldson and Patricia A. Werhane (Englewood Cliffs, N.J.: Prentice-Hall, 1979), pp. 11–24.
4. See the interview with Johnson and Johnson's president David R. Clare in David Freudberg, *The Corporate Conscience: Money, Power, and Responsible Business* (New York: American Management Association, 1986), pp. 239–48.
5. Freudberg, *Corporate Conscience*, p. 242.
6. Interview with Charles W. Powers in Freudberg, *Corporate Conscience*, pp. 67–68.
7. Donald Schön, *The Reflective Practitioner: How Professionals Think in Action* (New York: Basic Books, 1983).
8. The following characteristics are suggested by Charles W. Powers and David Vogel, *Ethics in the Education of Business Managers* (Hastings-on-Hudson, N.Y.: The Institute of Society, Ethics and the Life Sciences, The Hastings Center, 1980), pp. 40–45.

Chapter Three

1. Milton Friedman, "The Social Responsibility of Business Is to Increase Its Profits," in *Ethical Issues in Business: A Philosophical Approach*, ed. Thomas Donaldson and Patricia A. Werhane (Englewood Cliffs, N.J.: Prentice-Hall, 1979), pp. 191–97.
2. For a similar argument, see Charles W. Powers and David Vogel, *Ethics in the Education of Business Managers* (Hastings-on-Hudson, N.Y.: The Institute of Society, Ethics and the Life Sciences, The Hastings Center, 1980), pp. 16–18.
3. Charles E. Lindblom, *Politics and Markets: The World's Political-Economic Systems* (New York: Basic Books, 1977), p. 356.
4. J. Irwin Miller, "How Religious Commitments Shape Corporate Decisions," *Harvard Divinity Bulletin*, February-March 1984, p. 4.
5. Miller, "Religious Commitments," p. 4.
6. Miller, "Religious Commitments," p. 5.

Chapter Four

1. Barbara Ley Toffler, *Tough Choices: Managers Talk Ethics* (New York: John Wiley and Sons, 1986), pp. 103–4.
2. The ideas in this section are based on the discussion in John G. Simon, Charles W. Powers, and Jon P. Gunnemann, *The Ethical Investor* (New Haven, Conn.: Yale University Press, 1972), chapter 2.
3. Charles W. Powers and David Vogel, *Ethics in the Education of Business Managers* (Hastings-on-Hudson, N.Y.: The Institute of Society, Ethics and the Life Sciences, The Hastings Center, 1980), p. 44.
4. Simon, Powers, and Gunnemann, *The Ethical Investor*, pp. 22–25.
5. Michael Walzer, *Spheres of Justice: A Defense of Pluralism and Equality* (New York: Basic Books, 1983).
6. This definition of social harm in the international context is based upon Charles W. Powers, "An Assessment of the Questions We Ask of Economic Systems," in *Can the Market Sustain an Ethic?*, The 1977 D. R. Sharpe Lectures on Social Ethics (Chicago: The University of Chicago, 1978), pp. 68–69.

Chapter Five

1. These characteristics are suggested by Ralph Potter in relationship to policy debates about nuclear arms, but they are equally applicable in other settings. See his *War and Moral Discourse* (Richmond, Va.: John Knox Press, 1969), pp. 23–29.

Chapter Six

1. Oliver F. Williams and John W. Houck, *Full Value: Cases in Christian Business Ethics* (San Francisco: Harper & Row, 1978), p. 12.
2. William E. Diehl, *Thank God It's Monday!* (Philadelphia: Fortress Press, 1982), p. 75.
3. Diehl, *Monday!*, pp. 75–76.
4. William F. May, "The Virtues in a Professional Setting," The Third Annual Memorial Lecture of the Society for Values in Higher Education, Vassar College, Poughkeepsie, New York, August 6, 1984, p. 15.
5. This notion is suggested by remarks by William F. May, Cary M. Maguire Professor of Ethics, Southern Methodist University, at the National Consultation on Corporate Ethics, Center for Ethics and Corporate Policy, Chicago, Illinois, May 14, 1987. May suggests that the other cardinal virtues—courage, temperance, public spiri-

tedness—together with prudence can play a crucial role in responsible corporate leadership.

6. See, for example, the recent study by Robert N. Bellah et al., *Habits of the Heart: Individualism and Commitment in American Life* (Berkeley and Los Angeles: University of California Press, 1985).
7. Bellah, *Habits*, p. 72.
8. Bellah, *Habits*, p. 153.
9. Diehl, *Monday!*, p. x.
10. See, for example, Lawrence Kohlberg, "Education for Justice: A Modern Statement of the Platonic View," in *Moral Education: Five Lectures*, ed. Nancy F. Sizer and Theodore R. Sizer (Cambridge, Mass.: Harvard University Press, 1970), and Lawrence Kohlberg, "Stages of Moral Development as a Basis for Moral Education," in *Moral Education: Interdisciplinary Approaches*, ed. C. M. Beck, B. S. Crittenden, and E. V. Sullivan (New York: Newman Press, 1971).
11. Reinhold Niebuhr, *The Irony of American History* (New York: Charles Scribner's Sons, 1952), pp. vii–ix.

Chapter Seven

1. The following discussion of critical elements in strengthening ethical management is a revised version of a similar discussion in Michael Rion, "Corporate Responsibility: Advocacy from Within," in *Proceedings of the First National Consultation on Corporate Ethics*, ed. David A. Krueger (Chicago: Center for Ethics and Corporate Policy, 1986).
2. James O'Toole, *Vanguard Management: Redesigning the Corporate Future* (Garden City, N.Y.: Doubleday, 1985), p. 21.
3. Quoted in David Freudberg, *The Corporate Conscience: Money, Power, and Responsible Business* (New York: American Management Association, 1986), p. 7.
4. Barbara Ley Toffler, *Tough Choices: Managers Talk Ethics* (New York: John Wiley and Sons, 1986), p. 332.
5. The quote is taken from the official internal policy documents of a Fortune 500 company.
6. Freudberg, *Corporate Conscience*, pp. 200–201.
7. Freudberg, *Corporate Conscience*, p. 201.
8. Michael R. Rion, "Training for Ethical Management at Cummins Engine," in *Doing Ethics in Business: New Ventures in Management Development*, ed. Donald G. Jones (Cambridge, Mass.: Oelgeschlager, Gunn & Hain, 1982), pp. 27–44. This volume contains several examples of corporate ethics education programs.
9. The program is offered through the Center for Ethics, Responsibilities, and Values at the College of St. Catherine in St. Paul, Minnesota.

134   *Notes*

Wallace is director of the program and formerly vice-president for social policy, Northwest National Bank.

10. Peter T. Jones, "Sanctions, Incentives and Corporate Behavior," in *Corporations and the Common Good*, ed. Robert B. Dickie and LeRoy S. Rouner (Notre Dame, Ind.: University of Notre Dame Press, 1986), pp. 123–24.

11. "GE's Image Makes Conviction More Jarring," *Wall Street Journal*, July 5, 1985, p. 4.

12. William E. Diehl, *Thank God It's Monday!* (Philadelphia: Fortress Press, 1982), p. 176.

13. William E. Diehl, *Christianity and Real Life* (Philadelphia: Fortress Press, 1976), p. 78.

14. Alice Frazer Evans, Robert A. Evans, and William Bean Kennedy, *Pedagogies for the Non-Poor* (Maryknoll, N.Y.: Orbis Books, 1987).

15. This list is a composite from the suggestions by William Kennedy in chapter 10, "The Ideological Captivity of the Non-Poor," pp. 249–55, and by Robert Evans in chapter 11, "Education for Emancipation: Movement Toward Transformation," pp. 274–83, in *Pedagogies for the Non-Poor*.

16. Kennedy, "Ideological Captivity," p. 251.